CHAIN AND
BEAD JEWELRY
CREATIVE
CONNECTIONS

CHAIN AND BEAD JEWELRY

CREATIVE CONNECTIONS

NEW TECHNIQUES FOR
WIRE-WRAPPING
AND BEAD-SETTING

SCOTT DAVID PLUMLEE

WATSON-GUPTILL PUBLICATIONS / NEW YORK

Executive Editor: Joy Aquilino
Editor: Martha Moran
Art Director: Jess Morphew
Designer: Chin-Yee Lai
Production Manager: Alyn Evans
Photographers: Simon Lee; Scott David Plumlee

Published in 2009 by Watson-Guptill Publications,
an imprint of Crown Publishing, a division of Random House, Inc., New York
www.watsonguptill.com
www.crownpublishing.com

ISBN 13: 978-0-8230-2485-8

Library of Congress Cataloging-in-Publication Data

Plumlee, Scott David.
  Chain and bead jewelry creative connections : new techniques for
wire-wrapping and bead-setting / Scott David Plumlee.
      p. cm.
  Includes index.
  ISBN 978-0-8230-2485-8 (trade pbk.)
  1. Jewelry making. 2. Metal-work. 3. Beadwork. I. Title.

TT212.P54 2009
745.594'2—dc22
                                      2008044366

Cover Design: Chin-Yee Lai

Printed in China

First printing, 2009

1 2 3 4 5 6 7 8 9 / 17 16 15 14 13 12 11 10 09

ACKNOWLEDGMENTS

I wish to dedicate this book to everyone who believed in me, especially:

My loving parents, Larry and Shirley, for their encouragement and support
My brother, Jeff; his wife, Erika; and their two boys, Isaac and Nathan, for all the smiles
All the students who took workshops and encouraged me to write this book series
All the patrons who purchased my jewelry art and invested in my business
All the teaching institutions that invited me to lead jewelry-making workshops
All the fine art retail galleries that retail my jewelry and provide representation
Joy Aquilino and all the fine folks at Watson-Guptill/Crown/Random House
Tim Sheriff at Swanstrom Tools, for all the hard work on the mandrel-tip pliers
Anthony Squillacci at APAC, for making my findings and student supply kits
Judy and Richard Walker, for providing a writer's hideout in the hills of L.A.
Spencer Baum at Rio Grande, for all the digital images and catalog promotion
Sophie Lenoir, for the rooftop photo shoot to capture my face in front of Taos Mountain
Spider, for the technical proofreading and authentic Japanese 12-2 bracelet
Cynthia Eid, for all the technical information about working with Argentium
Teresa Fillman at Lortone, for the promotional tumblers to test and photograph

ABOUT THE AUTHOR

SCOTT DAVID PLUMLEE has been inspiring a new generation of chain jewelers over the past decade, publishing books and leading workshops nationwide. His previous book, *Handcrafting Chain and Bead Jewelry*, is a best seller in the jewelry-making field. A world traveler and jack-of-all-trades, Scott has studied ancient cultures and craft designs all over the globe and currently resides in sunny Taos, New Mexico.

"I challenge myself to create innovative chain designs by utilizing curiosity as a guide and creativity as a catalyst to find new solutions to the age-old question of how to combine silver and gemstones. Over the past decade, I have found that the path of least resistance in creating new designs is simply to be aware of the possibilities within the happy accident and explore my imagination with reckless abandonment. By employing creativity, I can turn the intangible images in my mind from sketchbook into sterling silver wire creations that are comfortable to wear and stunning to behold."

Scott David Plumlee

CONTENTS

PREFACE

Come exercise your bravado and explore beaded chain jewelry with me, as I lead you on a wire-working adventure. From a chaotic wire-wrapping approach to precise bead-embellishment techniques that are set into ancient chain patterns, this book has something to satisfy and challenge every level of jewelry artisanship. I'll show you how to set beads and assemble them into various chain designs and jump-ring techniques that connect them in interesting and innovative ways. For those of you curious enough to keep reading, let me tell you how I translated my creativity into the printed page.

Over the past two years, since the publication of my first book, *Handcrafting Chain and Bead Jewelry*, I have had a chance to travel the United States, leading over seventy jewelry workshops nationwide. This experience allowed me to test my teaching strategies for the craft of beaded chain design, fortifying me with a deeper understanding of how to teach others what I know and to measure student comprehension through in-class feedback to even the most challenging chain and bead techniques.

Along the way, I've found new approaches to old techniques, like rewriting the rules of wire wrapping by using an electric screwdriver to create "Chaos" beaded beads. I've also developed specialized mandrel-tip pliers to precisely set beads onto headpins, which alleviates some beaded chain frustrations. Modern science and technology have been explored to offer a variety of metal finishes, from patina darkening to a tumbled shine. I revisited ancient chain patterns with an eye on setting gemstone beads and developed a variety of unique ways to seamlessly connect metal chain and gemstone setting.

The first two chapters cover wire and bead basics and then continue into the essential chain-making and bead-setting techniques. These basics are developed more in the next two chapters, which feature "Chaos" and "Tornado" wire-wrapping techniques that progresses from simple earrings to embellished bracelets. More complex techniques are explored in the later chapters, where gemstone beads are used to embellish a variety of age-old chains, from the Byzantine, Flower, Japanese, Inca Puño, and European to the infamous six-sided Snake chain. I have designed beautiful gallery-quality jewelry projects that utilize each technique; all are presented in photo-illustrated, step-by-step instructions, rendering even the most difficult and complicated techniques understandable and doable.

The appendix outlines the basics of working with Argentium silver, and headpin making. There are illustrated chain configurations at the end of the book, which I think you'll refer to often, as well as a resource section that tells you where you can find all the tools, materials, and supplies used in the techniques and projects in this book.

Personally, the process of writing this book and creating the step-by-step images and text has been most rewarding, keeping my mind young and energized with each new problem to be solved. My self-challenge was to create innovative chain designs by using curiosity as a guide and creativity as a catalyst to find new solutions to the age-old question of how to combine metal and mineral. Patience and ingenuity transformed intangible images in my mind into notebook sketches then into silver wire creations that are comfortable to wear and stunning to behold.

I hope you get as much satisfaction using this book as I did in creating it.

1

CHAIN AND BEAD BASICS

The fundamental elements of beaded chain jewelry are metal wire "jump rings" and gemstone "beads," bedazzling components that only Mother Nature could provide. Before we begin working on techniques and creating jewelry pieces, we will explore a multitude of aesthetic options offered by different metal wires (red copper, yellow brass, brown bronze, karat gold, and Argentium sterling silver) and a variety of gemstone beads (yellow amber, purple amethyst, black onyx, blue quartz, red carnelian, green agate, and Venetian glass). And we'll cover all the hand and finishing tools you will need to marry metals and minerals, from mandrels, pliers, and calipers, to pickling pots and rotary tumblers.

WIRE

Metal wire is the essential component in chain making. It is a delicate balance between the malleable softness of the metal that allows a jump ring to be opened and closed without breaking and yet be strong enough to hold the jump ring's round shape and create a sturdy unsoldered chain. Pure metals are for the most part too soft for chain making, so we work with metal alloys, which are composed of several metals that have been melted together to produce a superior end product. Here are six metal alloys produced in wire form that I like to work with.

RED COPPER

Actually, copper is a pure metal, which becomes a brass when alloyed. In its pure form, it is quite inexpensive and readily available. Although copper is softer than sterling silver, it is invaluable for testing designs and for beginners to practice with. Eighteen-gauge copper round wire is available at your local hardware store. Look in the electrical wiring section to find 14-gauge copper round wire on a large spool; you may have to strip off the plastic insulation, but the price is right. Copper is a highly reactive metal that will turn black with exposure to the elements and will turn the wearer's wrist green as it oxidizes.

Copper wire

YELLOW BRASS

Brass is a family of alloys created by smelting copper and zinc together into a yellow metal that has a similar working characteristics to sterling silver. Yellow brass, also known as high brass, is achieved by smelting 70% copper with 30% zinc.

JEWELER'S BRONZE

Jeweler's bronze—also known as low brass, red brass, NuGold brass, pinchbeck, Dixgold, and Merlin's Gold—is composed of smelting 85% copper with 15% zinc. Jeweler's bronze is slightly darker than yellow brass with a rich warm color.

YELLOW, WHITE, OR ROSE GOLD

Gold wire is purchased in different karat (k) values that indicate its alloy composition. A karat number signifies the relative amount of gold in an alloy. For example, 24k gold is 100% pure gold, while 12k gold is 50% gold. Gold is alloyed with silver, copper, and other metals to achieve a desired color depending on its ingredients. Yellow gold is a combination of silver, copper, and gold. White gold typically combines nickel and gold, although there are white gold palladiums that are nickel free. Rose gold combines copper and gold.

When considering gold wire, keep in mind that it is quite expensive—fifty times more expensive than sterling silver. 14k gold is also denser than sterling silver by a factor of 1.48, thus more wire by weight is needed. Gold wire is sold by the pennyweight (dwt); twenty pennyweights equal one troy ounce (ozt). A cost-effective alternative is 14/20 gold-filled wire below.

Gold wire

14K GOLD-FILLED

14k gold-filled (GF) wire has a layer of gold alloy bonded to the outside of a base wire. With 14/20 GF wire, 1/20th of the wire's weight ratio is a thin layer of 14-karat gold that is heat and pressure bonded to the outside of a cheaper metal base wire, typically brass. Since the base metal is sealed within the bonded gold, it cannot leach out and tarnish the wire. If you want the look of gold without the huge cost, this option is ideal.

Gold-filled wire

Note: Gold plating is a thin layer of gold that has been electronically plated over a base metal. This technique is not advisable for chain making as the rings will rub together and quickly remove the gold layer.

ARGENTIUM STERLING SILVER

Argentium® sterling silver, invented by Peter Johns in 1996, is a relatively new silver alloy that lends numerous benefits to silversmithing over traditional sterling silver. Traditional sterling is 92.5% silver with the remaining 7.5% mostly copper. Argentium sterling is also 92.5% pure silver, but some of the copper has been substituted with a metalloid known as germanium. This small amount of germanium in the alloy, when heated, migrates to the surface, where it combines with oxygen to form a thin layer of germanium oxide. This layer of germanium oxide creates a barrier that prevents the copper in the alloy from oxidizing and darkening the silver's surface as traditional sterling would tarnish or antique.

This germanium oxide barrier also decreases reticulation, or wrinkling of the metal's surface, which allows the heated Argentium wire will pull up into a perfectly smooth teardrop-shaped ball. This same concept applies to the soldering process by preventing the darkening stains of "fire scale" from forming within the interior layers of the metal. The tarnish-resistance and fire-scale-free factors of Argentium sterling are why many silver-smiths are now using this modern marvel of an alloy, which has been dubbed "the way sterling was meant to be."

Argentium sterling silver wire

Tarnish Resistance

The most important reason I use Argentium sterling over traditional sterling is the tarnish resistance that proper heat treatment brings to my beaded jewelry designs. The longevity of the metal's ability to hold a polished shine and resist oxidation darkening is unparalleled. Point in case, a repeat customer who has such a high pH balance that he could turn a traditional sterling bracelet black in two weeks has yet to notice a color difference from his new Argentium sterling necklace after nine months of continuous wear.

Heat Hardening

The trick to obtaining the maximum tarnish resistance is to perform a precipitation-hardening process in your home oven to create the germanium oxide layer on the metal surface. (For more details, see page 19.) Place the finished jewelry (without magnetic clasps—they will demagnetize) in a clean, glass baking dish. Set to 450°F and bake for two hours.

Teardropping Headpins

The second greatest feature of Argentium wire is the ability to make perfectly smooth teardrop-shaped balls at the end of the wire. This ability allows the studio jeweler to create aesthetically pleasing head pins from any gauge of wire. (See page 155 for details on making your own headpins.)

Ductility and Malleability

Argentium has a greater ductility and malleability than traditional sterling silver. Ductility is the ability of a metal to be stretched or elongated, as when it's pulled through a drawplate (see page 26). Malleability is the ability of the metal to be transformed when forged with a hammer and anvil into a S-clasp (see page 32).

BEADS

Semiprecious gemstone beads have been used worldwide throughout history for personal adornment because they are visually arresting, physically long lasting, and are associated with a wide range of metaphysical properties. Once a status symbol of kings and queens, you can now find a mind-numbing assortment of gemstone beads at your local bead shop, craft stores, online, and through catalog companies (see page 157).

Beads by definition have a hole drilled through them so they can be strung together. Although there is no industry-wide standard for the size of the drilled hole, it typically ranges from 0.75mm to 1mm in diameter. Note that 20-gauge wire is 0.8mm, 19-gauge wire is 0.9mm, and 18-gauge wire is 1mm in thickness. If a headpin wire won't pass through a bead's hole, either use a smaller gauge headpin or enlarge the hole with a diamond-plated bead-reaming bit in an three-prong electric screwdriver (see page 17).

Gemstone beads, clockwise from upper right: carved jade, amber, carnelian, black onyx, amethyst, Venetian glass, blue quartz, and green agate (center).

Geology rates a gemstone's hardness on the Mohs scale, from 1 to 10, with 1 being soft talc and 10 being diamond hardness. I typically use gemstones with a 7 Mohs hardness, such as carnelian, amethyst, onyx, quartz, and agate, which are undamaged when polished with steel-shot in a rotary tumbler. Softer gemstones with 5–6 Mohs hardness, such as turquoise, lapis lazuli, and malachite, lose their shine with steel-shot but can be polished with rice in a rotary tumbler (see page 20).

Amber is not a mineral, but a translucent fossilized tree resin with organic inclusions that is millions of years old. This material is typically yellowish-gold with inclusions from oil residue, air bubbles, tree bark, and the occasional unlucky insect. The Beaded Flower Earrings (page 81) utilize a pair of 28mm golden-colored amber beads. Amber is much lighter than glass or gemstone, thus a larger bead can be used without creating too much weight.

Amethyst is a translucent purple quartz gemstone that can range from high-grade deep royal lavender to a low-grade pale lilac color. I use several sizes and shapes of amethyst beads throughout this book for different design applications.

The Beaded Infinity Chain Bracelet (page 38) uses 8mm faceted amethyst beads whose large size, rich color, and surface faceting allow them to stand on their own and complement the simple chain design. The Tornado-Wrapped Earrings (page 62) and Tornado Byzantine Bracelet (page 66) use simple 6mm amethyst beads whose smaller size and smooth surface allow them to be wrapped with gold wire and set into a more complicated chain design without overpowering it. The Beaded Inca Puño Bracelet (page 134) uses a large faceted nugget that tapers at both ends. The large bead creates a visually weighted centerpiece in the repetitive chain and tapers perfectly into the chain.

Black onyx is an opaque quartz gemstone with a glassy polish whose color is enhanced by saturating it in a boiling solution of cobalt chlorate, thus dyed from banded grays to an intense black. Opaque, black, smooth, and round, these beads can be a minimalist embellishment, allowing other elements of the design more significance.

The Power-Wrapped Beaded Chaos Bracelet (page 54) combines five 3mm black onyx beads with one 4mm red carnelian bead, a ratio that gives the single carnelian some companions while remaining the focal point, as the black absorbs and the red reflects. The Beaded Mobius Earrings (page 90) use three different sizes of black onyx beads in gradation throughout the repetitive chain pattern.

Blue quartz is a translucent quartz gemstone that ranges from natural sky blues to a variety of chemically enhanced regal blues. Blue, being my eye color, is one of my favorite embellishment hues. Unlike other common blue stones, such as turquoise and lapis lazuli, blue quartz is hard enough for steel-shot tumbling. It is also affordable and a good alternative to the more expensive options, like aquamarine or topaz.

The three blue quartz jewelry designs in this book illustrate differences between natural and enhanced blues. The Single-Flower Earrings (page 78) use natural 6mm x 7mm barrels; the off-round bead shape draws the attention, and the awe-inspiring hue holds the imagination. The Japanese 8-2 Key Fob (page 125) is finished with an eye-catching triplet of 10mm faceted beads. The Beaded Snake Chain Bracelet (page 146) uses faceted, round beads that were treated to enhance the color into a rich royal blue.

Carnelian is a translucent red quartz gemstone that can range from natural reddish-orange to heat-treated cherry red. Be-

cause iron is the coloring agent of carnelian, you can use a heat process to enhance the red color. This process was used on all the carnelian beads used in this book, giving them their consistent rich, cherry red color.

One 4mm carnelian bead, set with several 3mm black onyx beads, is the focal point of The Power-Wrapped Beaded Chaos Bracelet (page 54) and Embellished Chaos Earrings (page 49). The Beaded Mobius Bracelet (page 92) uses tube-shaped beads whose long, skinny shape allows them to be tightly packed, side-by-side, so they hang perpendicularly from the chain like fringe from a leather coat. The Beaded Dubious Bracelet (page 99) uses a series of round carnelian beads set onto silver headpin wires. The simple round beads echo the round balls of the headpins, allowing color to embellish the chain but not overwhelm its complex pattern. The beaded Twin and Triplet Bracelets (pages 112 and 115) use the same thin tube bead as the Mobius chain, but horizontally, stacked in a repeating fashion. Due to the thin diameter, the metal wire shows through the mineral, affecting its color—set with silver wire in the Mobius chain it looks strawberry red; set with gold-fill wire in the Twin Bracelet, it looks burgundy red.

Green agate is a translucent quartz gemstone that ranges from a murky green mixed with moss-like hornblende to a consistent verdant green color. The Beaded Flower Bracelet (page 82) uses twenty-two 6mm agate beads that were hand selected for consistency in color from three 16-inch strands or 198 beads. To complement this rich verdant color, I used gold-fill headpins and jump rings.

Venetian glass beads are handmade by skilled lampworking artisans in southern Italy. The Twinned Tornado Bracelet (page 119) features clear glass beads with a subtle blue swirl and tiny air bubble inclusions. I particularly enjoy the asymmetrical and imperfect quality of these handmade beads, which add depth to the jewelry design. Glass is translucent and lighter than most gemstones, which allows me to use larger glass beads without them being visually or physically heavy.

TOOLS

Any tool should be considered an extension of your fingers. Yet tools are specialized to perform tasks that your unaided fingers could not. An electric screwdriver is used to wrap wire into coils to be cut into jump rings. Different pliers are used to bend wire in precisely different ways, just as a hammer is used to flatten wire against an anvil. A common paperclip is key to the novice chain maker, just as the rotary tumbler is critical to the finished quality of your jewelry.

MANDRELS

A jump ring's inside diameter (ID) will be the exact same diameter as the mandrel used for wrapping the wire into a coil before it is cut into jump rings. Wire-wrapping mandrels are available in both millimeter and fractions-of-an-inch sizes. The chart (below) provides both millimeter and inch measurements to show how they compare. The left side lists diameters in ¼-mm (0.25mm) increments; the right side lists diameters in ¹⁄₆₄-inch (0.40mm) increments. The far right column lists the millimeter equivalent for each fraction-of-an-inch size.

A wrapping mandrel is a round metal rod that is used to wrap wire in a continuous coil before it is cut into individual jump rings. Aluminum knitting needles work great for wrapping, but don't use bamboo or plastic needles. Round aluminum knitting needles come in a wide variety of diameter sizes and are easy to find at your local knitting and fabric stores.

Note: Never trust the stated millimeter size on a package of knitting needles; instead, measure the needles with digital calipers. Try different brand names for varying needle sizes, and look for used knitting needles at garage sales or in your grandmother's knitting box for that elusive mandrel size.

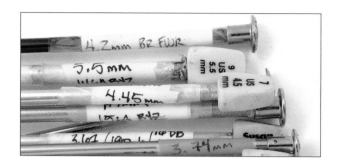

Knitting Needle Mandrels

I always measure my jump rings and mandrels with a digital caliper to 100th of a millimeter. I use knitting needle mandrels to wrap my wire into coils. For easy identification, I label each mandrel with its mm size.

Bending Mandrils

Convenient mandrels for bending earring backs are 7mm round wooden pencils and 8mm round plastic mechanical pencils. The 7mm pencil mandrel will also be used for bending the large loop of the S-clasp. For holding the small loops on the earring backs in some of the earring, we'll be using a 2.35mm steel rod mandrel.

Power Mandrels

This is a 3.6-volt electric screwdriver with a hex-base, three-prong chuck adaptor. You can buy the screwdriver in any hardware or home supply store, but the three-prong chuck must be ordered online (see page 157). This type of chuck holds a variety of mandrel sizes, and the space between the three prongs holds the end of the wire and maintains the spring tension as the coil is wrapped. Great for making coils, but we are also going to use it to spin wire into Chaos Earrings and bracelets in Chapter 3.

Millimeters	Inches	(metric size)
2mm	5/64"	(1.98mm)
2.25mm		
	3/32"	(2.38mm)
2.5mm		
2.75mm	7/64"	(2.78mm)
3mm		
3.25mm	1/8"	(3.18mm)
3.5mm	9/64"	(3.57mm)
3.75mm		
4mm	5/32"	(3.96mm)
4.25mm		
	11/64"	(4.37mm)
4.5mm		
4.75mm	3/16"	(4.76mm)
5mm		
5.25mm	13/64"	(5.16mm)
5.5mm	7/32"	(5.56mm)
5.75mm		
6mm	15/64"	(5.95mm)
6.25mm		
	1/4"	(6.35mm)
6.5mm		
6.75mm	17/64"	(6.75mm)
7mm		
	9/32"	(7.14mm)
7.5mm	19/64"	(7.54mm)
8mm	5/16"	(7.94mm)

Mandrel Size Chart

As an educator, I find that quality hand tools help to decrease frustration and increase the quality of my students' jewelry. To this end, I prefer American-made Swanstrom pliers because they are comfortable to use and will last a lifetime. Several tool supply companies are listed in the resources section on page 157.

Chain-Nose Pliers

Pointed chain-nose pliers are more appropriate for working with finer gauge wire and getting into a tight chain pattern to close that last pesky jump ring.

Flat-Nose Pliers

Two pair of short flat-nose pliers work in tandem to open and close jump rings with a broad grip on both sides of the jump ring.

Mandrel-Tip Pliers

I assisted Swanstrom Tool Company in developing these mandrel-tip pliers. One mandrel jaw is a consistent 3.1mm and the other jaw is a consistent 3.9mm diameter. This gives my students and me the ability to wrap perfect double loop bead settings. A second version of mandrel-tip pliers, which has a 3.5mm jaw and a 4.5mm jaw is also available.

Round-Nose Pliers

Typical round-nose pliers have tapered jaws, so you must keep the wire that is being bent at a specific place on the jaw to obtain a consistent diameter in a wire loop or double loop. Notice there are four marks on each tapered jaw, designating prescribed diameters. The tapered jaw ranges from 1mm to 5mm in diameter. The new mandrel-tip pliers replace the use of round-nose pliers for most of the bead-setting projects in this book, as they provide greater accuracy than round-nose pliers.

Side Cutters

Side cutters, aka flush cutters, are available in several sizes, each for a specific range of wire sizes. The smallest model is for wire up to 18-gauge, the medium model is for wire up to 14-gauge, and the largest is for wire up to 10-gauge thickness.

These tools, designed to simplify the jewelry-making process, should be thought of as extensions of your hands and eyes. Being a minimalist with tools and techniques allows the finished work to have a handcrafted look and feel.

Digital Calipers

Digital calipers are ideal for precise measurement of wire and mandrel diameters and the inside diameter of jump rings.

Felt-Tip Marker

You'll use a felt-tip marker to mark diameters on pliers' jaws and cutting lines on wires. Sharpie brand felt-tip markers can also be used as mandrels. They have a shaft that tapers from 12.25mm (at the middle of the marker) to 11mm (at the end of the marker).

Folding Lamp

Adequate lighting is key to seeing the subtle details of jump ring assembly.

Optivisors

Optivisors are magnifiers worn to help you focus on the fine detail of where a ring is being positioned within a chain pattern and to get a proper closure on each individual jump ring.

Wooden Hand Vise

A wooden hand vise helps to hold wire securely in its leather jaws by the lever-action from a triangular wooden wedge.

Measuring Tape

Fabric measuring tape, due to its flexibility, is perfect for measuring curved wire and can be cut to any length you need.

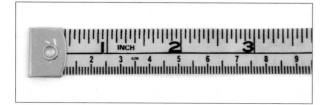

Paperclips

I give out lots of paperclips when I teach workshops, and I recommend that beginners start their chain design with a paperclip to identify a beginning point. You build the chain in a linear line, and when you drop it in progress (and you will), it is easy to identify where to continue the assembly.

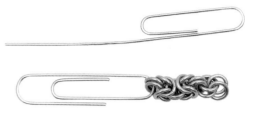

Flat Jewelry Files

Flat jewelry files are used to remove any burrs from the ring joint. Electrician's tape is used to make a handle on the flat file and to hold the cutter's set screw.

Sanding Pads

320-grit "superfine" sanding pads are used to smooth each jump ring's joint, as needed; this scuffing will polish out in the steel-shot tumbling, creating visually seamless rings. They are sold as 4 x 5–inch pads but can be easily cut into smaller 1 x 2–inch swatches.

Planishing Hammer

A planishing hammer is used, in conjunction with a bench block anvil, to flatten wire and to form S-clasps (see page 32).

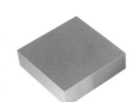

Bench Block Anvil

The bench block anvil sits on top of your work surface. It is made of steel and is generally about 4 x 4 inches and ¾-inch thick. Lay your wires on the anvil and gently tap with the flat side, or planishing side, of the hammer to flatten wire and with the ball-peen side of the hammer to texture the wire.

Frisbee

Frisbee disks are perfect for holding your beads, headpins, jump rings, and extra pliers during assembly, and when you take a break, or the phone rings, all the materials and tools for the project are in one location.

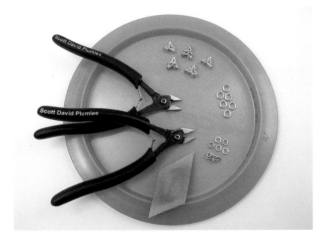

Storage Containers

You can store beads and rings in see-through stacking plastic bins and in plastic bags that zip shut. Metal rings are rough on plastic bags, so use 4mm thickness or freezer bags to prevent holes (and losing all your marbles).

FINISHING TOOLS, SUPPLIES, AND PROCESSES

I try to keep it low tech in my studio, but there are a few power tools and chemical processes that I use.

TARNISH RESISTANCE

The trick to obtaining the maximum tarnish resistance on Argentium sterling silver is to perform a precipitation-hardening process in your home oven. Place the finished jewelry in a clean, glass, baking dish. Set the oven to 450°F and bake for two hours. Once the metal is cool, the surface may appear to have a slight yellow tint owing to the reduction atmosphere of your oven. This film is quickly removed with a warm pickle solution (see below). You can then polish the metal to a high shine in a steel-shot-filled rotary tumbler (see page 20).

Hardening Argentium silver in a home oven.

Note: Not all semiprecious mineral type beads will survive heat processes. For example, magnetic beads lose their polarity during heating, and soft minerals, like turquoise and lapis lazuli, can burn in the heating process.

REMOVING SURFACE OXIDATION

A pickle pot is an acid-water solution that removes the surface oxidation from metal. You can use a small Crock-Pot with a ceramic liner, *but it is imperative that it is dedicated for non-food use ONLY and that you label the pot with a poison symbol*, such as a skull and crossbones. The dry grains of acid

Pickle pot and pickling acid

saturated with Black Max (below) and let the tumbler run for two weeks. The result for this bi-crown bracelet below was a brilliant gunmetal shine like hematite. If you take this journey, take care that you never reuse this tumbler body or shot for anything but this process, and wash your hands thoroughly after handling.

Tumbler, steel shot, and Black Max.
The brilliant gunmetal shine of this bi-crown bracelet is a result of tumbling sterling silver with steel shot and Black Max.

are available from a jewelry supply store; always add acid to water, following manufacturer's instructions. Using an electrical outlet timer, set the dedicated Crock-Pot for one hour to warm the solution and to turn off automatically after an hour. The solution will stay warm all day without risk of drying out. *Always use tongs to move jewelry in and out of the water or tie guide wires onto several bracelets and then dip them in.* If proper measurements are maintained, this acid solution should never get strong enough to actually burn you, but you still don't want it on your hands or clothing, nor dripping on your hardwood floor.

All jewelry and utensils should be neutralized with baking soda and rinsed under tap water after going through the pickle pot acid wash process. For those of you with more patience, you can seal the chain in a solution of pure lemon juice and/or fresh lemon wedges overnight. This will clean off surface oxidation similarly to the pickle pot acid wash. Whichever way you deoxidize your metal, it should be as rinsed and as clean as possible before you polish it in a steel-shot-filled rotary tumbler.

DARKENING METALS

Although treated Argentium sterling silver resists a patina, traditional sterling silver, copper, brass, and low-karat gold can all be darkened with liver of sulphur or by visiting your local mineral hot springs. A more permanent patina is produced by a product made by Midas and packaged by Rio Grande, known as Black Max. To test an interesting idea from chain guru Spider, I placed a traditional sterling bracelet and a handful of steel-shot in a dedicated tumbler with water

ROTARY TUMBLERS

Rotary tumblers, designed for polishing rocks into gems, can be used with stainless steel shot to produce a high shine on your finished jewelry designs. The rubber barrel is filled halfway with shot and two-thirds with water, just add your chain and a dab of soap and let it spin for at least thirty minutes. But if you leave it spinning for three days or even three weeks, you not only won't do any damage, but you will get an even stronger chain. The tumbling action of the steel-shot work hardens the metal like a thousand tiny hammers polishing the surface into a brilliant shine.

Lortone manufactures quality rotary tumblers in a variety of sizes and load capacities. This longer model can hold two or three barrels, allowing more options. For example, you could use one barrel with dry rice for polishing silver set with softer gemstones, a second barrel with water and steel-shot for polishing silver, and a third barrel dedicated to Black Max patina process.

If you need to tumble more than two or three bracelets at a time, you may want to opt for a larger motor and barrel size. This larger A4 model can handle three times as many silver bracelets and has a ten-sided (decagonal) interior that increases the tumbling action.

Some Tumbling Tricks of the Trade

- Use a metal coffee filter to strain the water from the shot and chain. You can reuse the tumbling water for a while, but when it turns black it is time to change it with fresh water.
- Make sure you purchase *stainless* steel shot or it will rust over time.
- Get a variety of steel-shot shapes, including balls and pins, for a superior polish to the whole chain.
- When not tumbling, your steel-shot should be sun dried or oven dried (150° F) and stored in an airtight container.
- When polishing loose unassembled jump rings, don't add steel-shot or you will spend hours separating the two materials. Instead just tumble the jump rings by themselves in water, or to speed up the process, tumble them with a three-ring interwoven "Flower" (see page 75) created from 10-gauge wire with a 1½-inch inside diameter.
- Use dry rice, without water, to tumble chains that have soft bead embellishments; the steel-shot will harm softer minerals like the blue lapis lazuli, turquoise, malachite, and hematite.

Jeweler's Journal

I keep an 8 x 10 journal documenting my jewelry design explorations. When inspiration hits, I loosely sketch necklace designs or chain patterns that have been forming in my mind's eye and then brainstorm, without pre-judgment, on various ways to create them. I spend extensive trial-and-error hours in the studio testing various solutions and keep detailed notes of all wire and ring measurements used in each experiment. If the design is successful, I can reproduce the entire process with the same results; if it still needs work, I can use the data to make educated decisions for the next experiment.

2

ESSENTIAL TECHNIQUES

• •

The essential component of chain making is the sizing of the individual jump rings that will be assembled link by link into a prescribed chain pattern. To help you understand the big picture of jump-ring theory, I will explain aspect ratio in simple language. We will then discuss how metal wire thickness is sized and go through an abbreviated tutorial on wrapping wire and cutting jump rings. With these basics established, I will list the appropriate inside diameter and wire thickness of the jump rings used in the nine chain patterns featured in the jewelry projects illustrated in this book.

• •

I'll next take you on a slow, precise, illustrated step-by-step course in proper jump ring and headpin utilization. Starting with the basics of jump rings—how to hold pliers, twist jump rings open, hook jump rings into a chain design, and, most important, how to close a jump ring flush and flat (with tips for left-handers)—we'll then explore using wire headpins to set gemstone beads with mandrel-tip pliers and the subtle nuances of wrapping a proper double-loop bead setting.

In the Beaded Infinity Chain Bracelet, we will assemble a dozen double loop bead settings into a simple two-on-one chain constructed of silver and bronze rings, with an option of adding copper Infinity rings to the completed two-on-one chain to create a stunning tri-metal bracelet. We will make a companion pair of Beaded Infinity Earrings, including detailed instructions on how to make matching earring backs by bending them simultaneously around a mandrel. Once you have understood, practiced, and mastered these skills, you will be ready to tackle all the beaded chain jewelry designs in this book with confidence.

jump ring's
inside diameter

wire
diameter

JUMP RINGS: THEORY AND PRACTICE

Chain jewelry is based on assembling individual metal jump rings, link by link, to create a linear length of flexible metal in a consistent pattern. The greatest frustration to the novice chain maker and expert jeweler alike is determining the correct size of the jump ring that will allow the successful assembly of a particular chain pattern. Each chain design has an established aspect ratio (AR) sizing (see page 27); if you use jump rings that deviate too far from the recommended AR sizing, the chain will be difficult to assemble, appear out of proportion (too tight or too loose), or both. The brass jump ring (below) illustrates the two key components of aspect ratio: the diameter of the wire's thickness and the jump ring's inside diameter (ID). Dividing the jump ring's ID by the diameter of the wire's thickness will give you the numerical value of the ring's AR. For example, a jump ring with a 4.5mm ID made from 16-gauge (1.3mm diameter) wire has an AR of 3.4 (4.5 ÷ 1.3 = 3.44). This information is critical, regardless of whether you choose to purchase jump rings or make your own. (For an overview of wrapping and cutting jump rings, see pages 26–27.)

PREMADE JUMP RINGS

If you choose to buy premade rings, be aware that each manufacturer has its own system for measuring them. Some measure the jump ring's inside diameter, while others measure its outer diameter. Some measure their jump rings in inches, some in millimeters; a few do both.

You should also note that jump rings are sometimes actually larger than the stated size of wrapping mandrel due to the "spring back" of the coiled metal. This spring-back effect occurs whenever wire is coil wrapped, but it is intensified when work-hardened wire is used, or when rings of large diameter are wrapped. For instance, 19-gauge wire wrapped on an 8mm mandrel will produce a jump ring that has 8.5- to 9mm inside diameter.

Jump rings

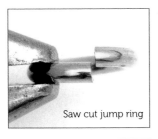

Saw cut jump ring

Kerfless jump ring

Jump rings can also be slightly smaller than the stated diameter of the wrapped mandrel when the coil is saw cut, which creates a *kerf*, or gap, in the circumference of the ring where it's cut from the coil. When the kerf is closed, it results in a slightly smaller—and slightly oval— ring. The thickness of the jump ring's kerf depends on the thickness of the saw blade, the technique used to cut it, and level of the manufacturer's quality control.

To overcome these inconsistencies when using purchased jump rings, I look for those that are "perfectly round" and "kerfless," and whose measurements are precise to $1/100$ of a millimeter, so that their closed ID is exactly as stated on the packaging. For a list of manufacturers, see the resources on page 157.

JUMP RING GAUGE

All the chain jewelry designs in this book are crafted from round wire, which is measured in thickness increments referred to as "gauges" by the American Wire Gauge (AWG) number system, which is also known as the Brown and Sharpe system. The European Union (EU) metric system measures wire thickness increments by millimeter (mm) diameters that are relatively close to AWG wires. Here is a table (above right) that lists AWG numerical gauge sizes and shows the cross-section size of the wire, the corresponding diameters in mm, and the EU metric system counterpart.

American Wire Gauge (AWG) sizes are most commonly sold in even numbers but can also be found in odd numbers. Almost all the chain designs in this book are crafted from 19-gauge round wire. Even when I had to draw my own 19-gauge through a drawplate, I found it to be a superior wire thickness to balance weight and strength. In my opinion, 18-gauge makes the chain too bulky, 20-gauge

AWG	dot	MM	EU
10	●	2.54	2.5
11	●	2.25	n/a
12	●	2.00	2.0
13	●	1.83	1.8
14	●	1.63	1.6
15	●	1.45	1.5
16	●	1.25	1.3
17	•	1.15	1.1
18	•	1.00	1.0
19	•	0.91	0.9
20	•	0.81	0.8
21	•	0.72	0.7
22	·	0.63	0.6
23	·	0.57	n/a
24	·	0.50	0.5

This chart shows wire thickness expressed in AWG numerical gauge, AWG gauge in millimeters, and European metric wire-measurement equivalents. The dots are the exact size of the corresponding wire diameters.

makes the chain too dainty, while 19-gauge looks and feels just right.

Beyond personal preference, any chain pattern can be constructed from any size of round wire, provided the correct diameter of jump ring is produced according to the chain's aspect ratio. When sizing any chain design up or down, keep in mind that the wire thickness and the strength of the metal you're using should be in balance. For example, 10-gauge sterling silver jump rings will be challenging to assemble because the wire is so thick and sterling silver is relatively hard to work; if you're going to work with such thick wire, it's best to work with a softer metal like fine silver, copper, or aluminum. Inversely, if you want to make a chain from very thin wire (22-gauge or smaller), you should make the rings from a harder metal like titanium or stainless steel, which is really strong but can be difficult to wrap.

Wire Drawing

Wire is shaped by a process called wire drawing, in which the wire is pulled through a drawplate, making the wire thinner and stronger and causing it to conform to the shape of the round hole within the plate. You can draw your own wire through a drawplate with pulling pliers, as shown. Wire can be purchased at different levels of hardness.

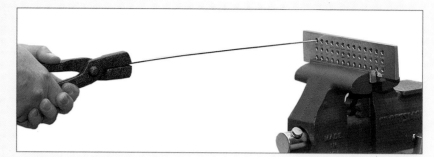

Dead-soft wire has been heat treated in an annealing process to reduce the stress within the metal. Half-hard wire has been pulled down four gauge sizes, and hard wire has been pulled down roughly eight gauge sizes. I recommend using half-hard sterling silver and hard brass wire for the correct balance between being too soft so that the rings deform and too hard so that the rings get brittle.

WRAPPING AND CUTTING JUMP RINGS

If you have the "do it yourself" spirit and want to make your own jump rings, knock yourself out. I have been wrapping and cutting my own rings over the past decade, but after working 290 troy ounces of silver wire in 2007, I hired a manufacturer to make my jump rings. The question you have to ask yourself is, "What is my time worth?" If you really don't have the time to make your own, just order premade jump rings and save yourself the inherent frustrations of the Aspect Ratio Blues. But if you want to make your own—here's an overview.

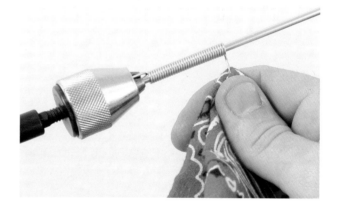

A 3.6-volt electric screwdriver and three-prong chuck are used to speed up the wire wrapping process; this technique also achieves a tighter and more consistent coil. Grip the wire with a cloth to dissipate the friction, and take care when you reach the end of the wire as it can cut your finger.

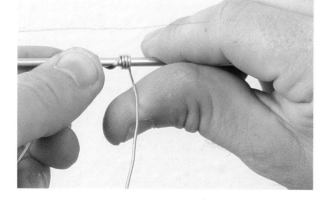

Although hand wrapping wire into a coil is a slow and laborious chore, it doesn't require any electricity, and it will strengthen your handshake. Wrapping wire requires hand-eye coordination to guide the wire into a continuous coil without introducing any gaps or overlapping the wire.

Cutting jump rings with side cutters

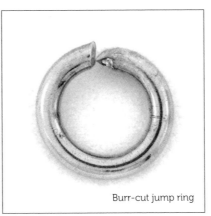

Burr-cut jump ring

Flush-cut jump ring

Jump rings can be cut from a coil with simple side cutters. The nipping action of the cutters leaves one side of the wire with a pointed burr and the opposite wire with a flat edge. If you want flush-cut rings, you must make two cuts per ring, cutting off a double-sided burr between each flush ring. Cutting jump rings by hand is time-consuming and requires hand-eye coordination to control the position of the cutter's blades to the coil.

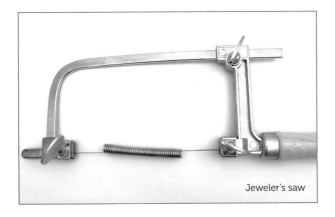

Jeweler's saw

A jeweler's frame saw and fine-toothed blades can increase your cutting speed and yield more consistent flush cut rings. Place the wrapped coil of wire onto the blade and then tighten the blade into the frame with the cutting teeth pointed inward. Place pressure with your thumb and first finger on the end six loops of the coil and saw them back and forth against the blade until they are cut off. Blade size #1 is appropriate for 20-, 19-, and 18-gauge wire; size #5 is suitable for 16-gauge; and size #6 for 14-gauge. Lubricating the blade with a wax product such as Bur-Life helps keep the saw blade cutting smoothly.

CALCULATING ASPECT RATIO

Below are a variety of chain patterns and their suggested aspect ratio (AR) sizing. I have listed all American Wire Gauge sizes from 20- to 14-gauge with their corresponding mandrel sizes to achieve the stated AR. The asterisks [*] indicate the jump ring sizes that are used in this book.

For chain configurations, see pages 158–159.

Note: You can make several different weaves with a single mandrel, provided that you use wire of different gauges. Inversely, if you have one gauge of wire you can make several weaves as long as you have different mandrel sizes.

DOUBLE CHAIN

AR = 2.85 to 3.0

The Double chain has a simple 2+2+2 assembly.

20-gauge (0.8) on 2.4mm or $^3/_{32}$-inch mandrel: AR = 2.93

19-gauge (0.9) on 2.75mm or $^7/_{64}$-inch mandrel: AR = 3.00

18-gauge (1.0) on 3.1mm or $^1/_8$-inch mandrel: AR = 3.0-3.1

17-gauge (1.14) on 3.25mm mandrel: AR = 2.85

*16-gauge (1.3) on 3.7mm mandrel: AR = 2.85 (used in Infinity chain)

15-gauge (1.45) on 4.25mm mandrel: AR = 2.93

*14-gauge (1.6) on 4.75mm or ¹³/₆₄-inch mandrel: AR = 3.03 (used in the Chaos bracelet)

BYZANTINE CHAIN

AR = 3.4 to 3.5

The Byzantine chain is also known as the "Birdcage," the "Idiot's Delight," and the "King's Braid."

20-gauge (0.8) on a 2.75mm or ⁷/₆₄-inch mandrel: AR = 3.44 or 3.46

*19-gauge (0.9) on a 3.1mm or ¹/₈-inch mandrel: AR = 3.44 or 3.53 (used in the Tornado Byzantine chain)

18-gauge (1.0) on a 3.5mm or ⁹/₆₄-inch mandrel: AR = 3.43 or 3.5

17-gauge (1.14) on a 3.9mm or ⁵/₃₂-inch mandrel: AR = 3.42

16-gauge (1.3) on a 4.5mm or ¹¹/₆₄-inch mandrel: AR = 3.46 or 3.36

*15-gauge (1.45) on a 4.9mm or ¹³/₆₄-inch mandrel: AR = 3.38 or 3.56 (used as a catch ring for S-clasps)

14-gauge (1.6) on a 5.5mm or ⁷/₃₂-inch mandrel: AR = 3.44

THREE-RING FLOWER CHAIN

AR = 4.3 to 4.4

The Flower chain is assembled from rings of two different sizes, but of the same gauge, in a sequential pattern—three interwoven Flower-size rings connected by two smaller Byzantine-size rings.

20-gauge (0.8) on 3.5mm or ⁹/₆₄-inch mandrel: AR = 4.3

*19-gauge (0.9) on 3.9mm or ⁵/₃₂-inch mandrel: AR = 4.29 or 4.35 (used in the Flower chain)

18-gauge (1.0) on 4.4mm or ¹¹/₆₄-inch mandrel: AR = 4.3 or 4.27

17-gauge (1.14) on 4.9mm or ¹³/₆₄-inch mandrel: AR = 4.3 or 4.53

16-gauge (1.3) on 5.5mm or ⁷/₃₂-inch mandrel: AR = 4.23 or 4.26

15-gauge (1.45) on 6.33mm or ¹/₄-inch mandrel: AR = 4.37 or 4.47

*14-gauge (1.6) on 7mm or ⁹/₃₂-inch mandrel: AR = 4.38 or 4.46 (used in the Infinity chain)

THREE-RING MOBIUS CHAIN

AR = 4.3 to 4.4

A Mobius chain is a repetition of three interwoven rings that are the same size as the rings in the Flower chain (above).

FOUR-RING MOBIUS CHAIN

AR = 5.4 to 5.5

The four-ring Mobius chain is a repeating four-ring Flower formation.

20-gauge (0.81) on 4.4mm or $^{11}/_{64}$-inch mandrel: AR = 5.43 or 5.38

19-gauge (0.91) on 4.9mm or $^{13}/_{64}$-inch mandrel: AR = 5.36 or 5.65

*18-gauge (1.02) on 5.5mm or $^{7}/_{32}$-inch mandrel: AR = 5.39 or 5.45

17-gauge (1.14) on 6.3mm or $^{1}/_{4}$-inch mandrel: AR = 5.53 or 5.57

16-gauge (1.3) on 7mm or $^{9}/_{32}$-inch mandrel: AR = 5.38 or 5.5

15-gauge (1.45) on 7.9 mm or $^{5}/_{16}$-inch mandrel: AR = 5.45 or 5.47

14-gauge (1.6) on 8.6 mm or $^{11}/_{32}$-inch mandrel: AR = 5.38 or 5.45

JAPANESE 12-1 CHAIN

This Japanese 12-1 pattern is used for the Twin, Triplet, and Twinned Tornado designs. The larger single rings are 15-gauge, 5mm ID rings and the two smaller rings are 19-gauge, 3.1mm ID (both same as the Byzantine chain, page 28).

JAPANESE 8-2 CHAIN

The Japanese 8-2 replaces the one large ring of the 12-1 with two-ring Flower formations, one made from two 19-gauge, 3.9mm ID rings (same as the Flower chain, page 28) and the other made from two 19-gauge, 3.1mm ID rings (same as the Byzantine chain, page 28).

INCA PUÑO CHAIN

AR = 4.3 to 4.4

The Inca Puño chain, also known as the "Box" chain or "Queen's Link," is a repetitive pattern of four rings folded into knot formations. It uses the same ring size as the three-ring Flower formation (page 28).

SNAKE CHAIN

AR = 3.8 to 3.9

The Snake chain, also known as Round Maille, Hexagon, and "Star Weave," is a repetitive six-sided chain.

20-gauge (0.81) on 3.1 mm or $^{1}/_{8}$-inch mandrel: AR = 3.82 or 3.91

*19-gauge (0.91) on 3.5mm or $^{9}/_{64}$-inch mandrel: AR = 3.83 or 3.91 (used in the Beaded Snake chain)

18-gauge (1.02) on 3.9mm or $^{5}/_{32}$-inch mandrel: AR = 3.82 or 3.89

17-gauge (1.14) on 4.4mm or $^{11}/_{64}$-inch mandrel: AR = or 3.86 or 3.83

16-gauge (1.30) on a 4.9mm or $^{13}/_{64}$-inch mandrel: AR = 3.77 or 3.97

15-gauge (1.45) on a 5.5mm or $^{7}/_{32}$-inch mandrel: AR = 3.79 or 3.83

14-gauge (1.63) on a 6.3mm or $^{1}/_{4}$-inch mandrel: AR = 3.87 or 3.89

WORKING WITH JUMP RINGS

A jump ring is a full circle of metal wire with a cut in the circumference that allows the jump ring to be twisted open, hooked into a chain, and then closed flush. Jump rings are the essential building block of any chain pattern; understanding how they are properly used and manipulated can be the difference between your finished chain jewelry lasting a lifetime or unraveling next week.

Note: Work with flat-nose pliers, one in each hand. Instructions are given for left-handers in steps 3 and 4.

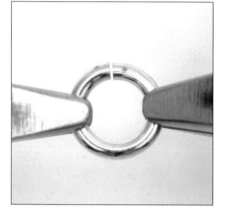

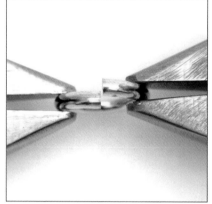

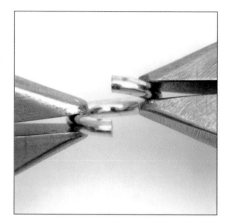

1 When holding a jump ring in your flat-nose pliers, the pliers' tips should be positioned at three o'clock and nine o'clock, keeping the opening of the jump ring upward at the twelve-o'clock position. This provides the best leverage on the ring and also keeps your elbows up, allowing you to use your whole upper body to open and close the jump ring, versus using just your wrists.

2 Looking down on the jump ring, notice that the right side is naturally higher than the left; this is due to the direction the wire was wrapped before cutting. This is a standard in the jump ring-making industry. If you make your own jump rings and inadvertently wrap the rings in an opposite spiral, don't worry—either direction works.

3 Twist the jump ring open by 30 degrees, *pulling* with the left pliers and *pushing* with the right pliers, both hands working simultaneously.

If you are left-handed, reverse this by pushing with the left pliers and pulling with the right pliers, both hands working simultaneously.

4 Since I am right-handed, I always twist open my jump rings with my dominate right hand pushing away, and my left, nondominant, hand pulling toward me. This lets me hold the open jump ring in my right pliers and feed the left side of the jump ring (painted red) through the chain design.

If you are left-handed, twist open your jump rings with your dominant left hand pushing away, and your right, nondominant hand, pulling toward you. This lets you hold the left side of the opened jump ring in your left pliers and feed the right side of the jump ring through the chain design.

5   Notice the red dot on the cut edge (left side) of the open jump ring; this is the end of the open ring that must hook through the chain opening.

6   As each new jump ring is linked onto the chain, focus on the end of wire (red dot) to help you find the angle needed to hook through the chain opening.

7   When closing each jump ring, remember that wire has memory. Use flat-nose pliers to grip both sides of the open jump ring, and bring the right tip below and just past the left tip to counterbalance the ring's memory of being twisted open the opposite way. *Slowly*, release your right-hand pliers' pressure, and the right side should snap into place with an audible click.

8   When the ring is closed properly, the closed edges are flush and the ring is even on both sides of the cut edges. Notice that the gaps between the jaws of the pliers line up, as shown, when the ring is properly closed. When working with shiny silver rings, looking for even, lined-up gaps can be an easier way to check for proper closure than checking the flush ends of the ring.

FORGING AN S-CLASP

When I started making chain, I could not find a clasping system that was sturdy and reliable and also aesthetically complemented my silver chain jewelry designs. Necessity being the mother of invention, I put a hammer to anvil for quite a while to "bang" out this signature S-clasp design.

Typically, bracelets and necklaces are fastened with a hook on one end of the chain and a catch ring on the other end. Many of the projects in this book are finished with an S-clasp (made from forged, S-shaped 14-gauge wire) that fastens through the catch ring.

Tools and Materials: To forge an S-clasp, the tools you will need are a planishing hammer and anvil, 7mm bending mandrel (pencil), side cutters, flat file, and measuring tape. The materials you will need are one 14-gauge silver wire cut into a 1¾-inch length and three 14-gauge silver jump rings (one attaches the S-clasp to the chain, two are assembled 1+1 as adjustable catch rings).

Note: For a review of bending and wrapping wire, see pages 26–27; for opening jump rings, closing jump rings, and adding/connecting jump rings, see pages 30–31. For tips for left-handers, see pages 30, 75, and 83.

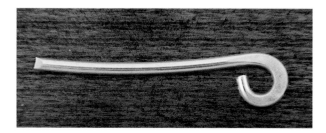

1 Using the side cutters, cut the 14-gauge wire into 1¾-inch lengths; one cut end will have a burr, and the other will be flat. Use the mandrel-tip pliers (3.1mm jaw) or round-nose pliers (at a 3.1mm diameter mark) and bend ½ inch of the flat end of the wire into a small single loop. Place the wire on the anvil and gently forge (flatten) the small loop with the hammer.

2 Forge the burr end of the wire into a tapering tongue shape—starting at the end, flatten about half the remaining wire length. Use a flat file to shape the wire's tip and a sanding pad to round it smoothly. Bend the tip of the flattened wire 45 degrees upward to create a "ski tip" to serve as the catch ring's gateway.

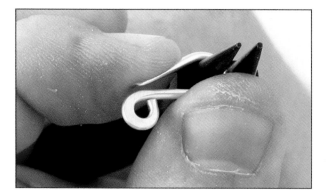

3 Use the round-nose pliers (marked at 6.3mm diameter) to grip the wire halfway between the ski tip and small loop and bend both ends of the wire toward one another equally till the bottom of the ski tip is touching the small loop, as shown.

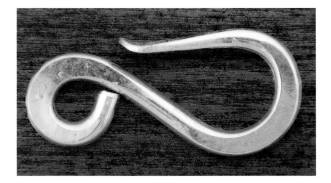

4 Lay the wire on the anvil and forge the remaining round wire, leaving the wire thicker toward both the small loop and the ski tip of the tongue. Straighten the clasp with pliers as necessary and adjust the large loop as necessary to allow passage of the 14-gauge ring.

5 Connect the small loop of the clasp to one end of the chain with the single jump ring. Add the 1+1 jump ring connection to the opposite end of the chain. Thread large loop of clasp through the end ring for a secure and alluring closure.

Another closure option, which can be used on any chain, is the magnetic clasp (see pages 130–131). Magnetic clasps are always added after the chain length is completed; otherwise the magnets will be attracted to your pliers and constantly be in the way during your jump-ring placement.

DOUBLE-LOOP BEAD SETTING

The double-loop bead-setting technique allows a gemstone bead to be securely held between the headpin's ball and the double loop of wire beyond the bead. The mandrel-tip pliers are used to create an exact inside diameter to the double loop, which allows the bead setting to be assembled into a variety of chain patterns. The double-loop bead setting is a critical technique that is used in most of the projects in the book, and it is a central, underlying concept that ties all the projects in this book together.

Tools and Materials: For this technique, the tools you will need are mandrel tip pliers (3.1mm) or round-nose pliers (marked at 3.1mm diameter) and side cutters. The materials you will need are one or more 1½-inch long, 19-gauge headpins (any metal), and one or more 6mm to 10mm beads (any stone or shape).

These headpins are manufactured from 2-inch long, 19-gauge 14/20 gold-fill wire (top left) and sterling silver wire (top right), and from 1½-inch long, 19-gauge 14/20 gold-fill wire (bottom left) and sterling silver wire (bottom right). A 2mm ball was soldered onto the end of each wire to form the headpin. To make your own headpins, see pages 155–156.

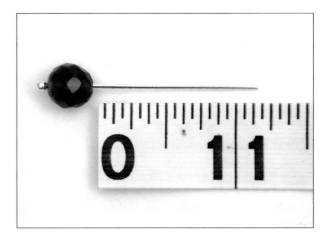

You will use 1½-inch headpins to set gemstone beads from 6mm up to 10mm in size for the double-loop bead-setting technique. (For larger beads, 10mm to 13mm, and to set magnetic clasps, you would need a 2-inch headpin.)

With an 8mm amethyst bead on the headpin wire, there is just over an inch of wire beyond the bead, which you will need to complete a full double-loop on a 3.1mm mandrel, with a slight tail of excess wire to trim off.

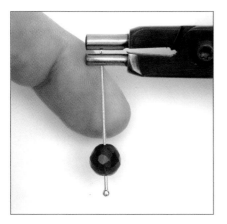

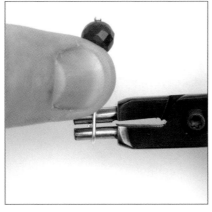

1 Grip the end of the 19-gauge headpin wire with the mandrel-tip pliers, keeping the 3.1mm mandrel jaw toward you. Keeping your finger pressure where the wire is bending, slowly bend the wire upward and around the 3.1mm jaw.

2 Bend the wire up around the 3.1mm mandrel jaw, stopping before the wire goes over the 3.9mm jaw.

3 Release the jaw pressure and allow the bead and balled end of the headpin wire to rotate back toward you to the beginning position.

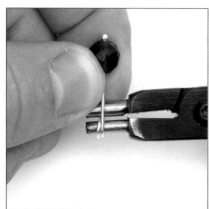

4 Regrip the wire with the pliers, keep your finger pressure where the wire is bending, and bring the head-pin wire upward, laying it to the right of the previously wrapped wire, wrapping inward toward the tool in a tight coil.

5 Bend the wire up and around the 3.1mm mandrel jaw, stopping before the wire goes over the 3.9mm jaw.

6 Release the jaw pressure and allow the bead and balled end to rotate back toward you to the beginning position.

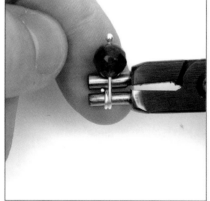

7 Regrip the wire with the pliers, keep your finger pressure where the wire is bending, and bring the headpin wire upward, laying the new wire to the right of the previously wrapped wire, wrapping inward toward the tool.

8 Bend the wire up and around the 3.1mm mandrel jaw, stopping before the wire goes over the 3.9mm jaw.

9 Release the jaw pressure and allow the bead and balled end to rotate back toward you to the beginning position.

10 Regrip the loops with the pliers and bend the remaining wire to bring the bead snug against the double loop.

11 With the 19-gauge wrapped loops snug against the bead, notice that the 19-gauge actually travels two and a quarter times around the mandrel. The excess beyond a full two rotations will be trimmed off.

12 With the side cutters, trim off the excess wire, keeping the flat side of the cutters against the bead and cutting the wire at a 45-degree angle, leaving the wire end with an angle. Just before you squeeze the side cutters to cut off the excess wire, place your finger over the excess to help prevent it from flying across the room. Save these silver scraps for recycling. Also, take care to cut through only one thickness of wire so you don't knick the next loop.

Practice, practice, practice—getting consistency with wire manipulation takes time and patience.

BEADED INFINITY CHAIN BRACELET

The Beaded Infinity Chain Bracelet is assembled as a simple two-on-one chain (1+2+1+2) with double-loop bead settings added onto each large silver ring. This chain design is then further embellished with copper rings that overlap each silver ring in an Infinity pattern. This simple jewelry pattern illustrates many of the key concepts of beaded chain design that will be expanded upon throughout this book.

Tools and Materials: To make this bracelet, the tools you will need are flat-nose pliers, mandrel-tip pliers (3.1mm) or round-nose pliers (marked at 3.1mm diameter), and side cutters. For an 8-inch bracelet, the materials you will need are eighteen 1½-inch long, 19-gauge silver headpins; nineteen 14-gauge, 7mm ID silver jump rings; thirty-four 16-gauge, 3.7mm ID bronze jump rings; thirty-six 19-gauge, 3.9mm copper jump rings; eighteen 8mm faceted amethyst beads; and a silver S-clasp or magnetic clasp.

Note: For a review of opening jump rings, closing jump rings, and adding/connecting jump rings, see pages 30–31. For tips for left-handers, see pages 30, 75, and 83. For 1+2+1+2 and Infinity chain configurations, see page 158.

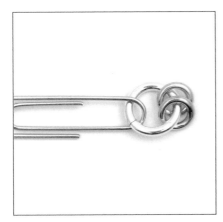

1 Always start any chain design with a paperclip to signify a beginning point so you build the chain in a linear line; when you drop the chain in progress, which you will, you will be glad to know where to start again.

2 Starting with the paperclip, use the flat-nose pliers to assemble the two-on-one chain using 14-gauge, 7mm silver rings connected by two 16-gauge, 3.7mm ID bronze rings in a repeating pattern. Continue into a bracelet length of chain (7 inches).

3 Open the first silver ring and replace the paperclip with an S-clasp (see page 32), and then add the first double-loop bead setting. Close this first large silver ring and notice that the headpin wire is spiraling downward and to the left. If you are using a magnetic clasp, add it at the end and begin with a paperclip.

4 Make eighteen double-loop bead settings (see page 34) with the amethyst beads and silver headpins. Open each large silver ring in sequence and add a double-loop bead setting, being consistent and making sure that each headpin is spiraling the same directions so that all the beads hang from the chain the same way.

5 Open and add one 19-gauge, 3.9mm copper ring through the left pair of bronze rings so it sits on top of the large silver ring.

6 Open a second copper ring and add it through the right pair of bronze rings and then hook it Bottom-wise (see page 83) through the previous copper ring to make an Infinity symbol on top of each large silver ring. Continue making the chain until you have an 7-inch length. Add the catch ring for the S-clasp (see page 32) or a magnetic clasp (see page 130).

BEADED INFINITY EARRINGS

The Beaded Infinity Earrings combine the previously mastered skills of double-loop bead setting and the interwoven Infinity pattern with the next skill of wrapping matching earring backs. The culmination of all of these skills will result in the gallery-quality beaded chain earrings, above.

Tools and Materials: To make these earrings, the tools you will need are round-nose pliers; flat-nose pliers; side cutters; mandrel-tip pliers (3.1mm) or round-nose pliers (marked at 3.1mm and 2.5mm diameters); one small (2.35mm) and one large (8mm) bending mandrel; and your hands. The materials you will need are two 2-inch long, 19-gauge silver headpins, for earring backs; two 1½-inch long, 19-gauge silver headpins for bead setting; two 14-gauge, 7mm ID silver jump rings; four 19-gauge, 3.9mm ID copper jump rings; and two 8mm faceted amethyst beads.

Note: For a review of opening jump rings, closing jump rings, and adding/connecting jump rings, see pages 30–31. For tips for left-handers, see pages 30, 75, and 83. For Infinity chain configuration, see page 158.

WRAPPING MATCHING EARRING BACKS

The principle behind a matching pair of earring backs is to bend both headpin wires at the same time, so that both earring backs will be identically shaped.

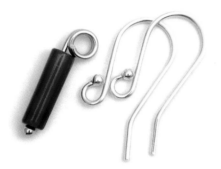

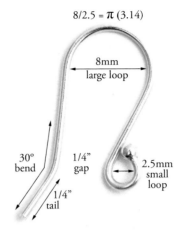

$8/2.5 = \pi \, (3.14)$

8mm
large loop

30°
bend

1/4"
gap

2.5mm
small
loop

1/4"
tail

The 2-inch headpins are necessary when setting beads larger than 10mm in size, as shown at left, where a 13mm red carnelian tube bead was set. On the right is a matching pair of earring backs formed from the 2-inch silver headpins.

This diagram illustrates the big picture of the earring backs design. Starting at the soldered-on 2mm ball, the headpin gets a 2.5mm small loop and then gets bent around a 8mm mandrel to form the large loop. As the large loop is being formed, the tip of the wire will come past the small loop by a quarter of an inch and then gets bent out 30 degrees. The overall earring shape has an aesthetic balance because the large and small loops are in a harmonious balance by being in proportion of pi (π) = 3.14.

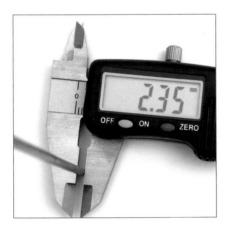

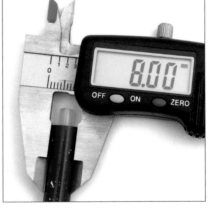

Here is a 2.35mm steel mandrel, available at your hardware store as a $^3/_{32}$-inch rod. This steel rod is typically sold in a 3-foot length, but all you need is a 5-inch length.

Here is a 8mm plastic mechanical pencil. If you can't find one, look in your hardware store for a $^5/_{16}$-inch steel rod or wooden dowel.

Finally, before we begin bending the earring backs, mark the jaws of your round-nose pliers, using an ultra-fine-point felt-tip marker, at a 2.5mm diameter.

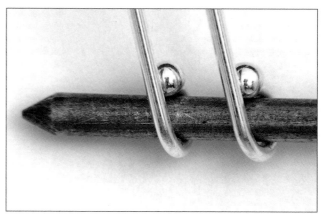

1 Grip the 2-inch headpin wire just below the soldered-on ball and bend the wire up around the round-nose jaw at the 2.5mm mark in a complete loop. Repeat this small loop bending with a second 2-inch headpin.

2 Add both small loops, facing the same way, onto the 2.35mm steel rod (smaller mandrel).

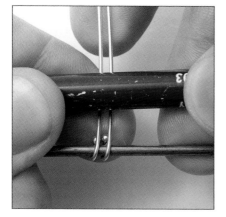

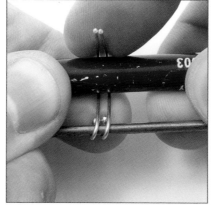

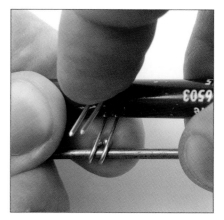

3 With the steel rod holding both wires, place the 8mm (larger) mandrel in front of the wires. Be sure to keep both mandrels parallel with a gap roughly the thickness of the larger mandrel.

4 While keeping both mandrels parallel and maintaining the gap between them, bend both wires over the large mandrel.

5 Bend both wires around the large mandrel, allowing the wire tips to travel past their small loops by a quarter of an inch, creating a tail that will help counterbalance the earring design.

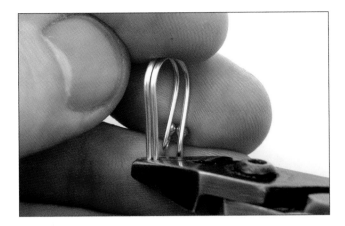

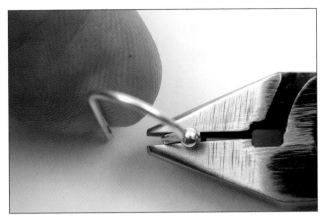

6 Remove both wires from both mandrels and then grip both ¼-inch wire tails in the flat-nose pliers. Bend both wires in a slight (30-degree) outward bend. This bend creates a safety stop to prevent accidental loss of the earring.

7 The finished earring back may need a pinch of straightening. Grip the small loop with the flat-nose pliers, look down on the wire, and adjust the form as needed.

FINISHING THE EARRINGS

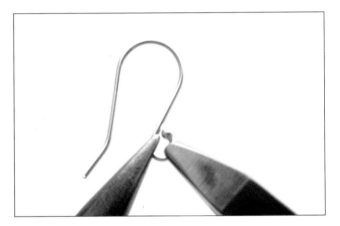

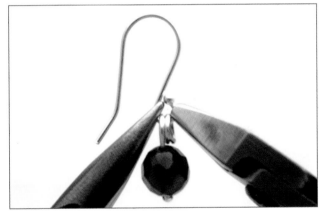

8 To add your earring design (bead setting) to the earring back, twist open the small loop just like a jump ring. Because the small loop has a limited surface area, I am using chain-nose pliers on the left and flat-nose pliers on the right.

9 To make the Infinity bead setting, create two double-looped amethyst beads using the 1½-inch silver headpins (see page 34). For each earring, use a 14-gauge, 7mm silver ring to connect the small loop of the earring back to the double loop of the bead setting; then connect the earring back to the double loop with two 19-gauge copper rings assembled 1+1 (see page 39, steps 5 and 6), over the single 14-gauge silver ring, creating two ring pairs. Follow steps 1–9 to make a matching earring. Try on earrings and look in the mirror to see if any adjustments need to be made.

3

"CHAOS" WIRE-WRAPPING

• •

This is an introduction to wire wrapping, covering a variety of quick and spontaneous methods for making unique and eye-catching silver beads that can be embellished with smaller semiprecious beads. These jewelry projects emphasize that wrapping and over-wrapping wire can create unplanned yet pleasing patterns that can look much like muscle fiber or a bird's nest.

We will start by making a pair of simple Chaos Earrings to explore the basic concepts of wrapping wire. Next, we will embellish the Chaos Earrings with a few 3mm beads on the outside of the Chaos wrapping to enhance its visual weight. The third Chaos Earring project will start with a 6mm bead on the headpin that will be nested inside the Chaos wrapping, much like an egg in a bird's nest.

The last project in this chapter, the Power-wrapped Beaded Chaos Bracelet, uses a 3.6-volt electric screwdriver to quickly wrap 22-gauge wire around a 14-gauge base wire to build a large wire-wrapped bead that can be embellished with 2mm and 3mm beads. I'll then show you eight different ways to connect the large Chaos beads, discussing the pros and cons of each method. Selecting which way to connect the beads is one of the fundamental aesthetic judgments a jewelry designer must face.

• •

HAND-WRAPPED SIMPLE CHAOS EARRINGS

The Chaos Earring designs will explore the basic concepts of wire wrapping. For this intro project we will simplify everything by just wrapping 22-gauge wire around the 19-gauge head-pin. For your convenience both wires will be held by the wooden hand vise, so you can concentrate on the how the wire feels to the fingertips, understanding that the wire has a memory of being straight, which causes the wire to spring back when bending.

Tools and Materials: To make these earrings, the hand tools you will need are a wooden hand vise, two chain-nose pliers, side cutters, measuring tape, and a 7mm wooden mandrel. The materials you will need are two 22-gauge silver wires cut into 8-inch lengths and two 2-inch long, 19-gauge silver headpins.

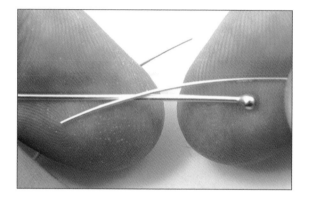

1 Start with the 19-gauge headpin and a length of 22-gauge wire. Overlap the wires, allowing ½ inch of the 22-gauge wire to pass over the 19-gauge headpin.

2 Place both wires inside the hand vise jaw. Close the hand vise and tighten its grip by forcing the wooden wedge toward the opposite end of the vise, keeping the wires overlapped.

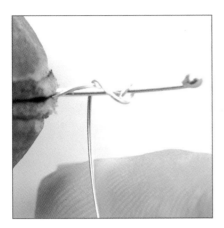

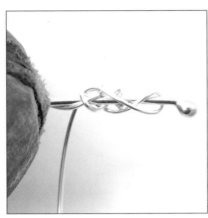

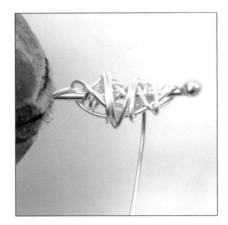

3 Begin wrapping the 22-gauge wire over the 19-gauge headpin, being careful not to push or pull with too much force or you will bend and distort the base headpin wire.

4 Continue to wrap and over-wrap the 22-gauge wire as crazy and chaotic as you like.

5 Build up the Chaos wrapping in length and girth. You should start to feel the spring-back effect of wrapping wire.

6 As the wire wrapping proceeds, try to concentrate a bit more girth toward the teardrop point of the 19-gauge headpin. This will give more visual weight to the bottom of the earring.

7 When you come to the end of the 22-gauge wire, bring it toward the wood hand vise so you can make a tight wrap around the base 19-gauge headpin.

8 Use the tips of your chain-nose pliers to tighten the end of the 22-gauge wire around the 19-gauge headpin, as any loose wire ends will snag loose clothing and catch hair.

9 With the Chaos wire wrapping complete, remove the 19-gauge headpin from the hand vise and tighten the wrapping with two pair of pliers—one holding the 19-gauge headpin and the other compressing the wrapped 22-gauge wire.

10 If needed, tighten the 22-gauge wire loop that is closest to the 19-gauge headpin's teardrop termination. This will prevent the Chaos wrapping from slipping off of the headpin.

11 Here is a pair of Chaos-wrapped headpins. Notice that they are as different as they are similar. No need to be a perfectionist with this technique—just allow the chaos to flow.

  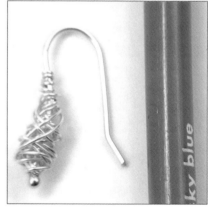

12 To bend the earring loop, hold both 19-gauge wire headpins against the 7mm wooden pencil and bend the wire in half. Bending both earring wires simultaneously will give you a matching pair that will hang the same from both earlobes.

13 Using the chain-nose pliers, grip the 19-gauge headpins ¼ inch from the tip of the wire and bend it slightly outward to allow easier passage through the earlobe.

The finished Chaos-wrapped earring.

EMBELLISHED CHAOS EARRINGS

The Embellished Chaos Earring design adds color and visual weight to the Chaos Earrings by incorporating several 2mm beads onto the 22-gauge wire at about halfway through wrapping the 8-inches of wire.

Tools and Materials: To make these earrings, the hand tools you will need are a wooden hand vise, two chain-nose pliers, side cutters, measuring tape, and a 7mm wooden mandrel. The materials you will need are two 22-gauge silver wires cut into 8-inch lengths; two 2-inch long, 19-gauge silver headpins; and ten 2mm beads (eight black onyx and two carnelian).

1 Begin the embellished Chaos earring the same as the Simple Chaos Earring design (see pages 46–47, steps 1–5) wrapping the 22-gauge wire around the 19-gauge headpin. Pause halfway through the wire wrapping (at step 5 on page 47) and add five 2mm beads (one red and four black, or vice versa) onto the 22-gauge wire.

2 Continue wrapping the 22-gauge wire, placing the 2mm beads into spaces within the previous wire wrapping. Try to place the beads all around the wire wrapping.

3 With the remaining 22-gauge wire, fill in the gaps between the 2mm beads. Finish the end of the 22-gauge wire tightly against the 19-gauge headpin. Repeat steps 1–3 for the second earring.

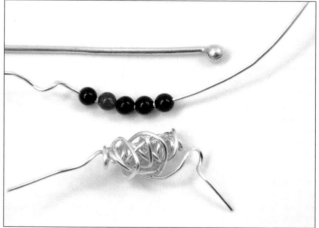

As with any wire-wrapping project, if you don't like your results, you can always unravel the wire wrapping to recycle the beads and headpin.

Notice that the 22-gauge wire wrapping will be bent and stiff due to the wire's memory of every bend; save this ball of wire and recycle.

NESTED CHAOS EARRINGS

The Nested Chaos Earring design starts with a 6mm amethyst bead on a 19-gauge headpin that is wrapped and over-wrapped with 22-gauge wire to build a nest around the bead, much like a bird's nest protects its eggs. This allows the color of the bead to peak through the wire wrapping, creating depth and intrigue.

Tools and Materials: To make these earrings, the hand tools you will need are a wooden hand vise, two chain-nose pliers, side cutters, measuring tape, and a 7mm wooden mandrel. The materials you will need are two 22-gauge silver wires cut into 8-inch lengths for wrapping the beads; two 2-inch long, 19-gauge silver headpins for both bead settings and forming earring backs; earring backs; and two round 6mm amethyst beads.

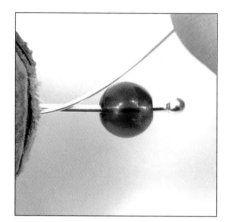

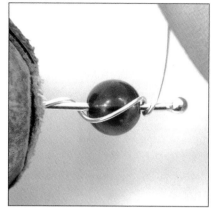

1 Start with a 6mm bead on the 19-gauge headpin. Overlap the 22-gauge wire on the headpin and place both wires in the wooden hand vise. Tighten the hand vise with the triangular wedge.

2 Wrap the 22-gauge wire once around the 19-gauge headpin and then diagonally over the 6mm bead, and then encase the bead with a few more wraps around the headpin wire.

3 Continue wrapping the 22-gauge wire back over the bead, being careful not to apply so much pressure that you bend the 19-gauge headpin.

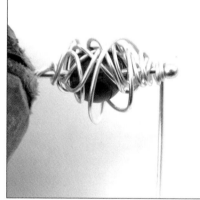

4 Allow the Chaos wrapping to form naturally; don't try to force a pattern.

5 The 22-gauge wire wrapping can be tighter or looser, as you prefer. Large loose wrappings need to be secured at either end with a tight wrap around the 19-gauge headpin wire or they will tighten as you continue to wrap.

6 When you come to the end of the 22-gauge wire, tightly wrap the tip of the 22-gauge wire around the 19-gauge headpin, toward the wood hand vise.

7 With the nested Chaos wrapping complete, remove the 19-gauge headpin from the hand vise and tighten the wrapping with two pair of chain-nose pliers, one holding the 19-gauge headpin and the other compressing the wrapped wire. Repeat steps 1–7 to create the second earring.

8 Bend the 19-gauge wire around a 7mm wooden pencil to form the earring back. Bending both earring wires at the same time will give you a matching pair that will hang the same from both earlobes (see page 48).

9 Using the chain-nose pliers, grip the 19-gauge headpin ¼ inch from the tip and bend it slightly outward to allow easier passage through the earlobe.

The finished Nested Chaos Earring.

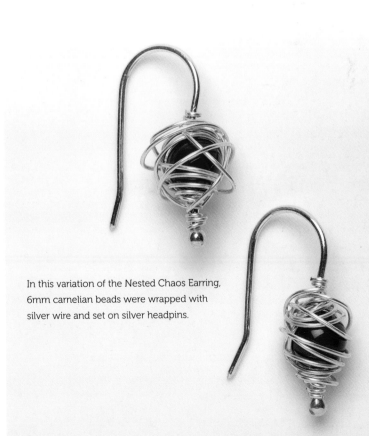

In this variation of the Nested Chaos Earring, 6mm carnelian beads were wrapped with silver wire and set on silver headpins.

POWER-WRAPPED BEADED CHAOS BRACELET

The beaded Chaos-wrapped bead technique allows you to quickly create wire-wrapped beads that are embellished with semiprecious beads, adding color to the implied motion. These wrapped, beaded beads are then combined with jump rings to create a unique bracelet with texture and pizzazz.

Tools and Materials: To make this bracelet, the hand tools you will need are a 3.6-volt electric screwdriver with a three-prong chuck, two flat-nose pliers, 3.9mm mandrel tip pliers (or round-nose pliers marked at 3.9mm), side cutters, measuring tape, fine-point felt-tip pen, and flat file. For an 8-inch bracelet, the materials you will need are six 14-gauge silver wires cut to 2-inch lengths for bead settings; six 22-gauge silver wires cut to 48-inch lengths for wrapping and overlapping bead settings; fourteen 14-gauge, 4.75mm ID silver jump rings; thirty 2mm black onyx beads; six 3mm red carnelian beads; and an S-clasp or a magnetic clasp.

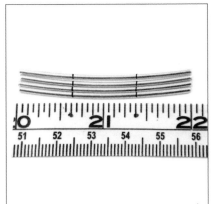

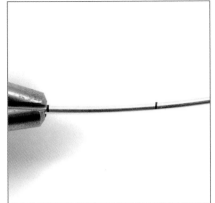

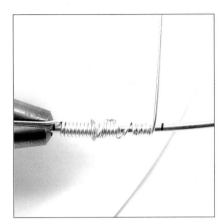

1 Cut the 14-gauge wire into 2-inch lengths. As you cut these lengths, trim off the pointed tip so both wire ends are flush. Use the flat file to slightly bevel the ends of the wire as they will show in the finished bracelet.

Use a fine-point felt-tipped marker to mark the wire at ⅝ inch in from both ends, allowing ¾ inch between the marks.

2 Insert the 14-gauge wire length into the three-prong chuck of the electric screwdriver, up to the first mark.

Note: Take care, because while wrapping the 22-gauge wire, you may inadvertently wipe off the second mark.

3 Insert the 48-inch length of 22-gauge wire into the three-prong chuck between two of the three teeth. Turn on the screwdriver, and start wrapping the 22-gauge wire around the 14-gauge wire length. Feel free to overlap the wraps as you go, but do not go past the second mark on the 14-gauge wire. Make two or three overlaps before you start adding beads.

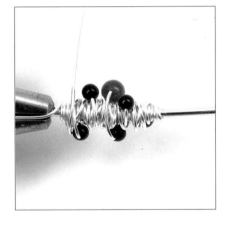

4 When you have wrapped roughly half of the 22-gauge wire, add six beads onto the loose end of the 22-gauge wire in the following order: three 2mm black onyx, one 3mm red carnelian, two 2mm black onyx beads.

5 To place the six beads on top of the previous wrapping, remove the three-prong chuck from the electric screwdriver and wrap the bead settings by hand so you can space them out equally along the length of the wire wrapping and all the way around the bead.

6 With the beads spaced equally, place the chuck back into the electric screwdriver, turn it on, and start wrapping the remaining wire over the beads to encase them within the wrapped wire.

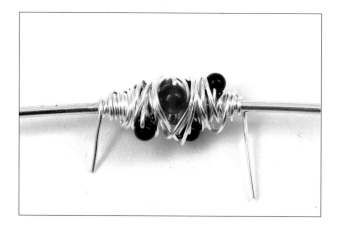

7   Finish the wire wrapping with the loose ends of the 22-gauge wire at opposite ends of the wrapping. Remove the 14-gauge wire from the three-prong chuck and finish both loose ends of wire by wrapping outwards, past the marks, over the 14-gauge wire. Use the chain-nose pliers to tighten the 22-gauge wire ends against the 14-gauge wire to prevent unraveling.

8   When you have finished wrapping, make sure that the 22-gauge wrapping is centered by measuring the length of bare 14-gauge wire on both sides, which should measure 1/2 inch on each side.

9   Grip one end of the 14-gauge wire with the mandrel-tip pliers and bend it around the 3.9mm mandrel jaw. Press this loop into the Chaos wrapping, bending some of the 14-gauge wire within the 22-gauge wrapping to create an S-shape.

10   Grip the opposite end of the 14-gauge wire with the mandrel-tip pliers and bend it around the 3.9mm mandrel jaw. Press this loop into the Chaos wrapping, bending some of the 14-gauge wire within the 22-gauge wrapping to create an S-shape. Connect the bead settings into an 7-inch bracelet length, using one of the following eight connection solutions. Once the beads are connected, add an S-clasp (see page 32) or a magnetic clasp (see page 130).

CHAOS CHAIN CONNECTIONS

One of the fundamental aesthetic decisions that any chain artist must make is how to connect individual wire-wrapped formations. In this section, I will take you on visual journey through eight different connection solutions, evaluating the pros and cons of each connection concept. My hope is for you to think outside the box—to realize that there are many different solutions to any given problem.

Solution 1: Connect the Chaos beads one-on-one, opening the loop on one bead and connecting it to another bead's loop. *Pro*: This is a simple and pleasing way to connect beads. *Con*: Each Chaos bead must turn 90 degrees as you connect them, so you only see the S-curve on every other bead. You will need an extra seventh Chaos formation for an 8-inch bracelet.

Solution 2: Connect each Chaos formation with a single jump ring. I used 14-gauge, 5.5mm ID jump rings. *Pro*: This solution allows each Chaos formation to lay the same way, creating a visual repetition of the S-shaped curves. *Con*: The gap between each bead is a visual weakness in the overall look of the bracelet.

Solution 3: Use a smaller diameter jump ring between each bead. *Pro*: A smaller jump ring closes the gap between the Chaos formations. I used 14-gauge, 4.75mm ID jump rings. *Con*: The smaller gap between beads looks better, but the single ring is still a visual weakness.

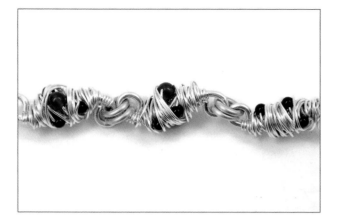

Solution 4: Add two jump rings between each Chaos formation. I used two parallel 14-gauge, 4.75mm ID jump rings. *Pro*: This solution adds visual and physical strength. *Con*: The connecting rings look kind of static, which does not complement the implied spiral of the Chaos formations.

Solution 5: Interweave two 14-gauge, 4.75mm ID jump rings between each Chaos formation. *Pro*: This solution works for me aesthetically as the interweaving of the two rings matches the implied spiraling motion of the formations. *Con*: I like this solution best, but I had more ideas I wanted to test, so I kept trying other approaches. In the end, I don't see a real con to this solution.

Side view

Top view

Solution 6: Interweave three jump rings between the beads. This is known as the Flower pattern (see page 74). I used three 14-gauge, 5.5mm ID jump rings. *Pro*: This solution is visually yummy, especially in this three-metal combination of brass, bronze, and silver. *Con*: I found that three 14-gauge jump rings barely fit the loop of the 3.9mm diameter of each Chaos formation, which ultimately limited the flexibility of the overall bracelet.

Side view

Top view

Solution 7: As in solution 6, interweave three jump rings between the formations in the Flower pattern, but use a thinner gauge wire. For this solution, I used 16-gauge, 5.5mm ID jump rings. *Pro*: This solution allows more physical flexibility throughout the bracelet length and the individual

Flower pattern sections are visually exciting. *Con*: The thinner wire of the connecting rings looks weak in comparison to the girth of the Chaos formations; but overall I think it is the second best solution.

Side view

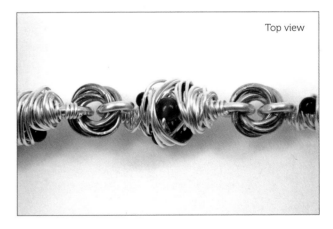

Top view

Solution 8: This solution also connects the formations with the spiraling Flower pattern but uses a fourth spiraling jump ring. For this solution, I used 16-gauge, 5.5mm ID jump rings. *Pro*: This connection is a visually exciting four-ring Flower formation and mimics the intensity of the Chaos beads. *Con*: The four-ring Flower formation visually competes too much with, and gives less prominence to, the Chaos-wrapped formations.

Now that we have taken this tour of trial and error, you may be asking which is the best solution? All eight solutions have their pros and cons, and you will see me use many of them throughout the book. I chose solution 5 for the finished Chaos Bracelet on page 54 because this method securely connects the Chaos formations without distracting from the intensity of each individual spiraling bead.

4

"TORNADO" WIRE-WRAPPING

• •

This chapter explores an exact wire-wrapping technique to encase and embellish gemstone beads that are held by the balled end of a 19-gauge headpin wire. These jewelry projects are beautiful examples of how the precise placement of fine wire can create an implied illusion of movement, like the spiral motion of a tornado's vortex. I first developed this wrapping technique by candlelight to calm my nerves while under a tornado warning when I lived in the flatlands of Kansas. It seems appropriate to name it after this awe-inspiring force of nature.

We start by making Tornado-Wrapped Earrings, one-wire earrings, where the same headpin wire that holds bead embellishment is also the earring back. We will then employ the mandrel-tip pliers to wrap double loops from the 19-gauge headpin wire, which will serve as the connector pair within a Byzantine chain, to create the Tornado Byzantine Bracelet.

• •

TORNADO-WRAPPED EARRINGS

The Tornado-Wrapped Earrings are unique in design as a one-wire earring, where the same headpin wire that holds the wire-wrapped bead embellishment is then bent into the earring back. With the 6mm bead on the 19-gauge headpin wire, a length of 24-gauge wire is wrapped and overlapped around the bead, adding visual depth and the perception of motion.

Tools and Materials: To make these earrings, the hand tools you will need are chain-nose pliers, side cutters, measuring tape, 8mm round mandrel, and a bandana to protect your hands from the friction of the wire. The materials you will need are two 24-gauge gold wires cut into 4½-inch lengths for wrapping the beads; two 2-inch long, 19-gauge silver headpins for the earring backs; and two 6mm purple amethyst beads.

Note: The 24-gauge wire spirals in a continual direction, either clockwise or counterclockwise. This keeps all the wraps and overlaps tight against the bead; if you do not keep the wire wrapping in a continual direction it will become quite evident, as the previous wire wrapping will begin to unwrap.

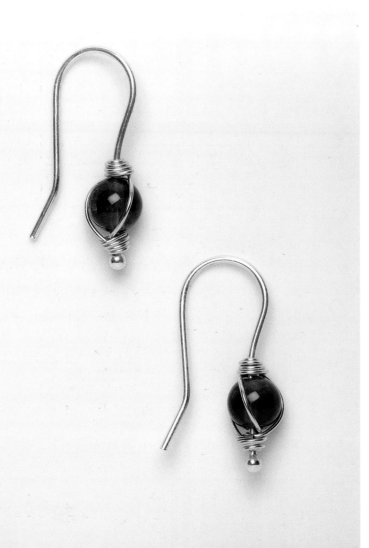

I purposely buy dead-soft 24-gauge gold-fill wire so that I can harden and straighten it (without losing flexibility for hand wrapping) by bending the wire slightly with repeated hand pulls through a through a folded bandana. To start, uncoil 3 feet of wire and hold one end with the flat-nose pliers in your nondominant hand. Using a folded bandana to reduce friction, as shown, pull the wire with your dominant hand. Begin each pull at the pliers, guiding the wire with the bandana hand, and pull evenly to the wire's end. With each pull, adjust your thumb position to bend the wire against the curve created by the previous pull. On the final few pulls, equalize the thumb-to-first-finger pressure so the wire is pulled straight. It should be quite a bit springier than before.

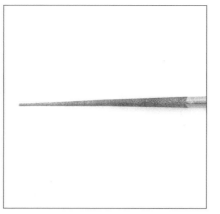

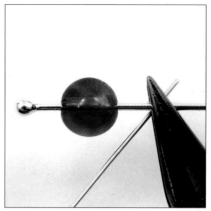

To create matching earring pairs, lay out matching pairs of beads (on their headpin wires) onto a small pillow to see how many earring pairs can be crafted from each mineral, and to make sure that the beads will allow the 19-gauge wire to pass through them.

If the hole within the bead does not allow the 19-gauge wire to pass through, the hole *can be* enlarged with a bead-reaming tip (shown above) held in the 3-prong chuck of an electric screwdriver. I find this anywhere from easy to impossible to do, depending on the hardness of the mineral.

1 Use the chain-nose pliers to hold the 24-gauge wire on top of and against the 19-gauge wire. Position the 24-gauge wire length at a 45-degree angle to the 19-gauge wire, leaving 1/8 inch of 24-gauge wire above the intersection of the two wires.

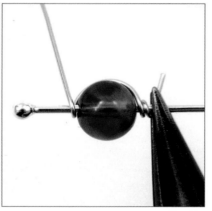

2 Wrap the 24-gauge wire one and a half times around the 19-gauge base wire, keeping a tight coil.

3 While pushing the bead toward the previous wrap held by the pliers, bend the 24-gauge wire diagonally over the bead and wrap it around the 19-gauge base wire.

4 Continue wrapping the 24-gauge wire around the 19-gauge base wire, completing two full loops.

Finish the first tail of 24-gauge wire (created in step 2) by wrapping it in a double loop around the 19-gauge headpin; trim off any excess wire with the side cutters.

5 Bend the 24-gauge wire diagonally over the bead, making the second pass over the bead, on the opposite side from the first pass.

6 Bend the 24-gauge wire one full loop around the 19-gauge base wire just beyond the previous double loop, completed in step 4.

7 Continue wrapping the 24-gauge wire, overlapping the previous wrap, for a total of three revolutions. This triple wrapping will gradually move downward toward the bead and gradually get larger in diameter.

8 After three full loops, bend the 24-gauge wire diagonally over the bead, making a third pass over the bead.

9 Bend the 24-gauge wire one full loop around the 19-gauge base wire, just beyond the previous double loop, completed in step 4.

10 Continue wrapping the 24-gauge wire, overlapping the previous wrap, for a total of three revolutions. This triple wrapping will gradually move upward toward the bead and gradually get larger in diameter.

11 After completing three full loops, trim off any excess wire, and bend the tip of the remaining 24-gauge wire inward.

12 To hide the wire end, use the tips of the chain-nose pliers to gently press the bent tip of the 24-gauge wire into the gap between the bead and the 24-gauge wire that passes over the bead.

13 Repeat steps 1–12 to make the second, identical Tornado wrapping.

14 Form the top of the shepherd's hook by bending the middle of the 19-gauge headpin wire around a 8mm mechanical pencil mandrel until the pointed tip and teardrop are almost touching (left).

Grip ¼ inch of the pointed wire tip with the chain-nose pliers and gently bend the tip outward (middle) to give a graceful curve to the shepherd's hook earring back. Hold the top of the shepherd's hook and bend the bead wrapping slightly outward to give a smooth hourglass shaped to the overall earring form (right).

Tip: To keep matching pairs of earrings together through the final steel-shot tumbling process, run a length of fine fishing line through a gap on each earring. You'll find the gap between the bead and the 24-gauge wire that passes over the bead.

TORNADO BYZANTINE BRACELET
WITH DOUBLE-LOOP BEAD SETTING

To assemble the Tornado-wrapped bead embellishments into the Byzantine chain, you will wrap the 19-gauge headpin wire into a double loop, which will substitute for every other connector pair (see illustration at top of next page) within the Byzantine chain. To keep the double loop at a consistent 3.1mm inside diameter, I developed special mandrel-tip pliers with the Swanstrom Tool Company. Start with 1½-inch long, 19-gauge headpins, because you'll need 1 inch of the 19-gauge wire beyond the Tornado wire embellishment for the 3.1mm-diameter double loop.

Tools and Materials: To make this bracelet, the tools you will need are mandrel-tip pliers (3.1mm) or round-nose pliers (marked at 3.1mm diameter), two flat-nose pliers, two chain-nose pliers, and side cutters. For an 8-inch bracelet, the materials you will need are seventeen 1½-inch long, 19-gauge silver headpins to double-loop and Tornado wrap the beads; seventeen 24-gauge gold wires cut into 4½-inch lengths to Tornado wrap the beads; 172 19-gauge, 3.1mm ID jump rings (thirty-six in silver [connector rings] and 136 in gold [knot formation rings]); two 15-gauge, 5mm ID catch rings; seventeen 6mm amethyst beads; and an S-clasp or a magnetic clasp.

Note: For a review of opening jump rings, closing jump rings, and adding/connecting jump rings, see pages 30–31. For tips for left-handers, see pages 30, 75, and 83. For the Byzantine chain configuration, see page 158.

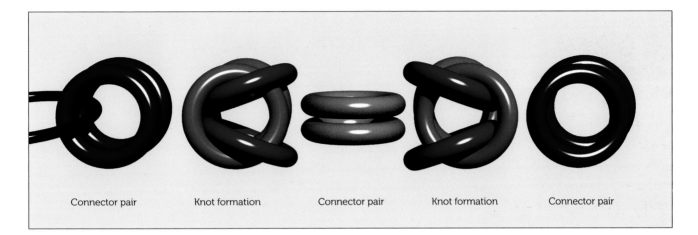

Connector pair   Knot formation   Connector pair   Knot formation   Connector pair

The illustration above shows the Byzantine chain separated into its two components: the connector pairs (shown in blue and gray) and the knot formations (shown in red and green). The four rings of the knot formation are assembled two-on-two and then folded back and angled open to create a rectangular opening within the knot formation that is fulfilled and connected to the next knot by the connector pair of rings.

When assembling the Tornado Byzantine Bracelet, each bead setting's double loop will replace every other connector pair of rings (shown in blue) in the chain, while the alternating connector pair of rings (shown in gray) will be utilized to connect the knot formations into the Byzantine chain. Please refer to this illustration while following the bracelet construction instructions.

1 Using the 4½-inch, 24-gauge gold wires and the 1½-inch headpins, Tornado-wrap seventeen beads, following the instructions for the Tornado-Wrapped Earrings on pages 63–65, steps 1–13. You will need at least 1 inch of 19-gauge wire beyond the 24-gauge wire-wrapped bead to complete the double loop to set the bead (see step 2).

2 To make the double loops on the Tornado-wrapped beads, follow the instructions for the Double-Loop Bead Setting on page 35.

ASSEMBLING THE TORNADO BYZANTINE BRACELET

Now that you've set all seventeen Tornado-wrapped beads with double loops, you are ready to assemble them into the Byzantine Bracelet Chain. In assembly, each double loop will replace every other connector-ring pair within the Byzantine chain (see above). This requires that you first assemble the knot formations on each side of the bead settings and then connect the knot formation with connector pair rings.

1 Start with seventeen Tornado-wrapped, double-loop bead settings. Onto each bead setting, add four 19-gauge, 3.1mm ID gold rings (the first two rings of knot formation). Add four more 19-gauge gold rings to the four rings just added (the third and fourth rings of the knot formations), connecting the rings 2+2 on each side of the double-loop bead setting.

2 On the knot formation, fold back the outer gold rings and angle open the inner gold rings to reveal the rectangular opening within the first knot formation. This knot formation can be held open with a paperclip as you add the next two rings in step 3. Make seventeen of these beaded knot formations, following steps 1 and 2, but add the paperclip to only one of the beaded knot formations.

3 Using the knot formation with the paperclip, add two 19-gauge, 3.1mm ID silver rings (connector pair) through the knot formation, replacing the paperclip. Add one 15-gauge 5mm silver ring to this connector pair to serve as the beginning point of the chain, as shown. This ring will be the catch ring in the clasping system.

4 Line up several knot formations assembled in step 2, making sure all the double-looped headpin wires are angled the same way for consistency in the chain. In this example, the balls of both headpins angle toward the large catch ring.

Fold back the outer gold rings and angle open the inner gold rings of the knot formations on both sides of the Byzantine chain to be connected, as shown.

5 Add one silver connector ring through the rectangular opening within the knot formations, connecting the formations into a chain. Add this first silver connector ring to assemble all seventeen Tornado-wrapped beads by their adjoining knot formations. You'll add the second silver connector ring of the pair following steps 1–9, on pages 69–70.

Adding the Second Connector Ring

Adding the second connector ring is easier said than done, so I am slowing down the process to help alleviate the inherent frustrations of the pliers gymnastics this requires.

1 Using chain-nose pliers, first open the second silver connector ring 30 degrees and hook the left side of the ring through the first knot formation above the first silver connector ring (added in step 5).

Notice that the pliers and the jump ring remain stationary, and your fingers bring the chain around the ring.

2 To make it easier to get the left-side tip of the connector ring into the second knot formation, gently twist the chain clockwise, and then bring the connector ring's tip through the second knot formation.

3 The connector ring's left-side tip is peeking through the second knot formation. Be sure to keep the open connector ring pointed upward so the second knot formation does not slip off the ring as you work. Because the connector ring is angled open by 30 degrees, it is difficult to get your chain-nose pliers on the left side of the connector ring to close it.

4 To begin closing the second connector ring, place the chain-nose pliers on top of the right side of the open second connector ring and below the already-closed first connector ring (added in step 5 above) and gently squeeze the ring to 10 degrees.

5 Gently squeeze the open ring till it almost touches, but not with so much pressure that you scratch or nick the ring.

Note: If the joint of the first ring is where you are applying pressure, you may twist this first, closed ring open slightly. Rotate it around so you are not pressing against the joint of the first ring.

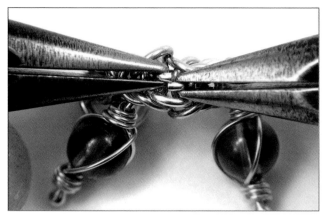

6 Now you can grip both sides of the almost-closed connector ring with two chain-nose pliers, one on each side of the ring's joint.

7 Bring the right side of the ring below the left side to counter the wire's memory, bringing the tips past one another, as shown, so they have a spring tension against one another.

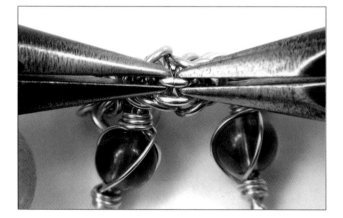

8 Allow the right side of the ring to spring back (usually with an audible click). Both ends of the ring should lay flush and flat against one another, without gap or offset.

9 Here are two beaded knot formations that have been assembled with connector ring pairs. Combine the next beaded form starting at step 5 on page 68. Add the second connector rings to the entire chain length, following steps 1–8 above. To complete the Tornado-Byzantine Bracelet, add an S-clasp (page 32) or a magnetic clasp (page 130).

This variation of the Tornado-Byzantine Bracelet
features blue lapis beads on a silver chain with an
S-clasp closure.

5

THE FLOWER CHAIN

This chapter focuses on the interweaving of two or more jump rings to create a spiral of rings that can combine bead settings in new and visually intriguing ways. We will explore the sequential pattern of the age-old Flower chain, which alternates two parallel rings between three interwoven rings in the Flower Chain Bracelet. These spiraling Flower formations will then be infused with gemstone bead settings, singularly in the Single-Flower Earrings and then sequentially in the Beaded Flower Earrings. We will build on these basic techniques by alternating double-loop bead settings with the spiraling three-ring Flower formations down a linear length to create the amazing Beaded Flower Bracelet.

THE FLOWER SPIRAL

This is a practice exercise that will help you perfect the Flower spiral, which you will use in the jewelry projects later in the chapter.

Tools and Supplies: For this practice exercise, you will need two flat-nose pliers and three 14-gauge, 7mm ID jump rings (one each in silver, gold, and copper). Since this is a practice exercise, feel free to use whatever wire gauge size you have, wrapped according to the Flower aspect ratio of 4.3 (see page 28).

Note: For a review of opening jump rings, closing jump rings, and adding/connecting jump rings, see pages 30–31. For tips for left-handers, see pages 30, 75, and 83. For Flower Spiral configuration see page 158.

The key to achieving consistent spiraling of jump rings is to always open each jump ring the same way. Since I am right-handed, I make a habit of opening each ring pushing my right pliers forward and pulling my left pliers toward me. When connecting rings, I hold the right side of the open jump ring in the pliers and feed the left side of the jump ring (which is facing me, as shown) into the chain toward me, where I can see it clearly.

If you are left-handed, twist open your jump rings with your dominant left hand pushing away, and your right, nondominant hand, pulling toward you. This permits you to hold the left side of the opened jump ring in your left pliers and feed the right side of the jump ring through the chain design.

1 Start by closing the first ring, shown in copper.

2 With the first (copper) ring closed flush, add the second (silver) ring, pushing its open left end from the backside and through the center of the first ring.

3 Close the second (silver) ring flush.

4 Add the third ring (gold) the same way you added the ring in step 2, pushing it through the centers of the first and second rings. Close the gold ring flush.

The finished Flower formation. Notice that all three rings lay into one another as they spiral in the same rotation. Once you've mastered this technique with large rings, practice with smaller rings: Three 19-gauge, 3.9mm ID jump rings.

FLOWER CHAIN BRACELET

The Flower chain is a sequential pattern where the Flower forms are separated with a connector pair of jump rings that allows all the Flower forms to face the same direction. The rings in the connector pair remain parallel to each other and do not spiral between each Flower form, and they are a smaller diameter than the rings used for the Flower.

Tools and Materials: To make this bracelet, the tools you will need are two flat-nose pliers and chain-nose pliers (optional) for closing those pesky third rings. For an 8-inch bracelet, the materials you will need are eighty-seven 19-gauge, 3.9mm ID jump rings for the three-ring interwoven Flower formations (twenty-nine each in silver, gold, and copper); fifty-six 19-gauge, 3.1mm ID silver jump rings for the connector rings between the Flower forms; two 15-gauge, 5mm ID silver catch rings; and a silver S-clasp or a magnetic clasp.

Note: For a review of opening jump rings, closing jump rings, and adding/connecting jump rings, see pages 30–31. For tips for left-handers, see pages 30, 75, and 83. For Flower chain configuration, see page 158.

Note: Although only silver rings were used in this bracelet, this chain pattern can be made from any single metal or mixed metals. I sometimes used different metal rings in the steps to emphasize the chain construction details.

1 Start with the Flower Spiral formation assembled on page 75. Add one 15-gauge, 5mm ID silver jump ring through the center of all three Flower rings, to serve as a beginning point. On the other side of the Flower form, add two 19-gauge, 3.1mm ID silver connector rings through the centers of all three rings in the Flower.

2 Add the first (copper) ring of the next Flower through the silver connector pair added in step 1.

3 Add the second (silver) ring of the next Flower through the same connector pair and then behind and through the center of the first (copper) ring, added in step 2.

4 Add the third (gold) ring of the next Flower through the same connector pair and then behind and through the center of the first and second rings, added in steps 2 and 3, to complete the triple-interwoven Flower formation.

5 Add two silver connector rings through the centers of all three rings of the Flower made in steps 2–4.

6 Continue the sequential pattern of Flower form, connector pair, Flower form, connector pair to complete a 7-inch chain length. Add an S-clasp (see page 32) or a magnetic clasp (see page 130) to create an 8-inch bracelet.

SINGLE-FLOWER EARRINGS

The Single-Flower Earrings combine the previous elements of the Flower formation, the double-loop bead setting, and the shepherd's hook earring backs. This is a good intermediate project to get you comfortable with the interweaving of three rings onto the double loop of the bead setting before we attempt the more demanding assembly of the Beaded Flower Bracelet (page 82).

Tools and Materials: To make these earrings, the hand tools you will need are two flat-nose pliers, mandrel-tip pliers (3.1mm) or round-nose pliers (marked at 3.1mm diameter), and an optional pair of chain-nose pliers for getting that pesky third gold ring closed. The materials you will need are two 1½-inch long, 19-gauge silver headpins for double-loop bead settings; two 2-inch long, 19-gauge silver headpins for the earring backs; six 19-gauge, 3.9mm ID jump rings (two each of gold, silver, and copper) for the Flower formations; and two barrel-shaped 6mm blue quartz beads.

Note: For a review of opening jump rings, closing jump rings, and adding/connecting jump rings, see pages 30–31. For tips for left-handers, see pages 30, 75, and 83. For Flower Formation configuration, see page 158.

1 Make two double-loop bead settings (see page 35), making sure to match the colors of the stones. Add the first (copper) ring of the Flower formation through the double-loop of the bead setting.

2 Add the second (silver) ring of the Flower formation, bringing the ring from the backside through the center of the copper ring and then through the double loop of the bead setting.

3 Close the silver ring without letting it unwind from the first (copper) ring. Notice how the silver rings spirals around the copper ring.

4 Add the third (gold) ring from behind and through the center of the copper and silver rings and then through the double loop of the bead setting.

5 Close the gold ring without letting it unwind from the other two rings and the double loop to complete the triple interwoven Flower formation.

6 Make and then add the earring back (see page 41) to each bead setting by twisting open the small loop of the earring back, just like a jump ring, hooking it through all three rings of the Flower formation and then closing it with the headpin's ball touching the 19-gauge wire.

7 Make a matching earring, following steps 1–6.

Put the earrings on and look at them in a mirror. Critique the design and the way they feel and hang. Think about any changes you might want to make—a different hook shape, a smaller or larger bead, a longer chain to dangle, etc. Make a sketch in your journal. Earrings should be viewed as small sculpture installations.

BEADED FLOWER EARRINGS

The Beaded Flower Earrings are a continuation of the previous Single Flower Earrings but with an extended Flower chain that allows the bead embellishment to swing more as it dangles from the ear.

Tools and Materials: To make these earrings, the hand tools you will need are two flat-nose pliers, mandrel-tip pliers (3.1mm) or round-nose pliers (marked at 3.1mm diameter), and optional chain-nose pliers for getting that pesky third ring closed. The materials you will need are two 1½-inch long, 19-gauge silver headpins for double-looping bead settings; two 2-inch long, 19-gauge silver headpins for the earring backs; eighteen 19-gauge, 3.9mm ID jump rings for the Flower formations (six each of gold, silver, and copper); eight 19-gauge, 3.1mm ID gold jump rings for the connector pair rings; and two 8mm round amber beads.

Note: For a review of opening jump rings, closing jump rings, and adding/connecting jump rings, see pages 30–31. For tips for left-handers, see pages 30, 75, and 83. For Flower chain configuration, see page 158.

1 Create a Flower formation following steps 1–5 of the Single Flower Earrings (pages 78–79).

2 Add two 19-gauge, 3.1mm ID gold connector pair rings onto the Flower formation made in step 1, passing them through all three rings of the Flower. Keep the connector rings parallel to each other.

3 Build the next three-ring Flower formation using copper, silver, and gold 19-gauge, 3.9mm ID rings, spiraling through the gold connector pair you attached in step 2.

4 Add two gold 19-gauge, 3.1mm ID connector pair rings onto the Flower formation added in step 3.

5 Build the next three-ring Flower formation onto the connector pair added in step 4.

6 Continue alternating Flower formations and connector pairs until the earring is the length you desire. Then add an earring back (see page 41). Make a matching earring, following steps 1–6.

BEADED FLOWER BRACELET

This Beaded Flower Bracelet utilizes a continuous pattern of 6mm beads to embellish the Flower chain. The connector pairs used in a typical Flower chain (page 74) will be replaced here with the double loop of a 19-gauge, 3.1mm ID headpin; each will hold a 6mm bead. Because the connector pairs are now double-loops, the design pattern will be assembled using three-ring Flower formations between the beaded double loops.

Tools and Materials: To make this bracelet, the hand tools you will need are two flat-nose pliers, mandrel-tip pliers (3.1mm) or round-nose pliers (marked at 3.1mm diameter), and optional chain-nose pliers for getting that pesky third ring closed. For an 8-inch bracelet, the materials you will need are eighty-seven 19-gauge, 3.9mm ID jump rings for the Flower formations (twenty-nine each in gold, silver, and copper); twenty-two 1½-inch, 19-gauge gold headpins for the double-loop bead settings; two 15-gauge, 5mm ID gold catch rings; twenty-two 6mm round black onyx beads; and a gold S-clasp or a magnetic clasp.

Note: For a review of opening jump rings, closing jump rings, and adding/connecting jump rings, see pages 30–31. For tips for left-handers, see pages 30, 75, and 83. For Flower chain configuration, see page 158.

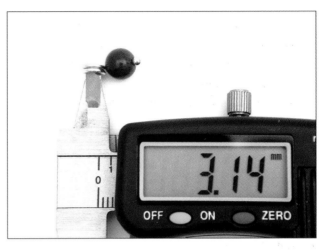

Set all twenty-two of the 6mm beads by double looping each 19-gauge headpin with the 3.1mm jaw of the mandrel-tip pliers (see page 35). If you are using traditional round-nose pliers, make a mark at the 3mm diameter, and keep all your looping a bit larger than the 3mm mark or you won't be able to pass the third ring though it in assembly.

When in doubt, always double-check the double loop's inside diameter with digital calipers. The ID will always be a pinch bigger than the mandrel because of the metal wire's mechanical spring-back.

Tips for Consistent Spiraling: Bottom-wise and Top-wise Techniques

Please review the proper way to open, close, and add jump rings (pages 30–31).

Attaching a jump ring to a Flower formation: The first variable in consistent spiraling is to be consistent about the way you open and add jump rings. Open a jump ring: *For right-handers*, while holding the right side of the jump ring with the right-hand pliers, feed the left tip of the jump ring into the Flower formation counterclockwise. *For left-handers*, feed the right tip of the jump ring into the Flower formation clockwise. If you are ambidextrous, either way will work; just make sure you always feed the rings the same way.

The Bottom-wise/Top-wise decision: The second variable of consistent spiraling requires more conscious thought. It is a concept that I refer to as the "Top-wise or Bottom-wise" decision. After the tip of the open jump ring travels though the beginning double loop, you need to bring this same tip through the center of the previously added ring for them to spiral. You'll have to decide whether you bring the jump ring's open tip from the *top* down through the center of the previously added Flower ring, or from the *bottom* up through the center of the previously added Flower ring. Both ways are just as easy, and just as difficult. I did all the projects in this book in the Bottom-wise fashion, pointing up against gravity. No matter how you decide to spiral your rings, all three rings of each Flower formation need to spiral the same way, and all the Flowers of the chain need to spiral the same way. So find what's best for you and stick with it.

1 To create a starting point, attach a paperclip to a double loop of a bead setting with a copper jump ring. Connect the bead settings, one by one, with single (copper) jump rings. For a consistent pattern, as the chain progresses make sure that all the beads are added to the same side of the chain and that you keep all the double-looped headpin wires spiraling in the same direction. Continue for 3 or 4 inches of this chain before you add the second and third Flower rings.

2 For steps 2–7, start at one end of the chain and work in a linear direction. Add the second (silver) jump ring to each Flower formation, parallel to the (first) copper ring. If you hold the right side of the open jump ring in the right-hand pliers, the left side of the open jump ring will travel from right to left through the starting double loop.

3 The left tip of the silver jump ring will then hook behind the copper ring and travel Bottom-wise up through the center of the copper ring. The silver ring stays stationary as you swivel the chain around the ring.

4 The left tip of the silver jump ring will then travel from left to right through the next double loop. To prevent the silver ring from unspiraling from the copper ring before you close it, turn the silver ring upward, so gravity doesn't cause it to slip back through.

5 Close the jump ring tight. Use flat-nose pliers to grip both sides of the open jump ring, and bring the right tip below and just past the left tip. *Slowly* release your right-hand pliers' pressure, and the right side should snap into place with an audible click.

6 With the silver rings in place, the chain will start to tighten up and minimize the spacing between the beads. *Warning:* The gold jump ring (to be added in step 7) may be difficult to add, and impossible to add if the double loops have an inside diameter smaller than 3mm, so feel free to stop here.

7 Add the third (gold) jump ring to each Flower formation, keeping it parallel to the copper and silver rings. Holding the right side of the open jump ring in the right-hand pliers, the left side of the open jump ring will travel from right to left, through the starting double loop.

8 The left tip of the third (gold) jump ring will then go behind the copper and silver rings and travel Bottom-wise up through the center of both. Ever-so-slightly twist the chain clockwise, swiveling it around the gold ring (while keeping the ring stationary).

The left tip of the gold jump ring will then travel through the next double loop from left to right. Turn the ring up to prevent it from slipping out of the copper and silver rings.

9 Grip the left tip of the gold jump ring with the pointed chain-nose pliers and close the ring almost tight.

10 Close jump ring tight (see page 84, step 5). This is the hardest ring to close, but it can be done.

Here is the finished triple-interweave beaded Flower chain, ready for you to add the S-clasp (see page 32) with a single 15-gauge, 5mm ID ring between the S-clasp and the ending beaded Flower formation. Or add a magnetic clasp (see page 130).

6

MOBIUS AND "DUBIOUS" CHAINS

· ·

This chapter explores the ropelike effect of a repeating Flower pattern, known as the Mobius chain. Unlike the Flower chain, the Mobius chain has no connector pair rings between the Flower formations. We will use the Mobius pattern to assemble a Mobius Chain Bracelet of spiraling silver rings, cascading three-bead, tri-metal Beaded Mobius Earrings, and a striking Beaded Mobius Bracelet that weds the Mobius chain with a multitude of long, barrel-shaped carnelian beads. The Masculine Mobius Bracelet project will explore a substantial, weighty, four-ring Mobius chain, followed by a brass and silver bracelet made in the Dubious pattern of four rings separated into two spiraling pairs. The final project in this chapter, the Beaded Dubious Bracelet, demonstrates how to set gemstones into a twisting chain pattern and then how to neutralize the twisting by alternating the ring-assembly angles, so the bracelet lies flat on your wrist.

· ·

MOBIUS CHAIN BRACELET

The Mobius chain is basically a repeating Flower chain with no connector pair rings between each Flower formation. By definition, a true Mobius strip is a wide ribbon of material that twists as it makes a complete circle, so there is no true inside or outside to the ribbon. The chaining community has used the terms *Flower* and *Mobius* for any spiraling of jump rings, so I am using the terms as follows: A Flower chain is sequential pattern with a connector pair between each spiral, and a Mobius chain is a repeating pattern without a connector pair between each spiral.

Tools and Materials: To make this bracelet, the hand tools you will need are two flat-nose pliers and optional chain-nose pliers for getting that pesky third ring closed. For an 8-inch bracelet, the materials you will need are 171 19-gauge, 3.9mm ID silver jump rings for the Flower formations; two 15-gauge, 5mm ID silver catch rings; and a silver S-clasp or a magnetic clasp.

Note: For a review of opening jump rings, closing jump rings, and adding/connecting jump rings, see pages 30–31. For tips for left-handers, see pages 31, 75, and 83. For Mobius chain configuration, see page 158.

Note: Although only silver rings were used in this bracelet, this chain pattern can be made from any metal or mixed metals. I sometimes used different metal rings in the steps to emphasize the chain configuration details.

The finished Mobius chain creates a tight pattern with a more masculine and rope-like feel than the Flower chain.

1 Start with one large, 15-gauge, 5mm ID silver catch ring and then add the first Flower formation, shown in silver, gold, and copper (see page 75).

2 Add the first silver ring (copper) of the next Flower form through the three rings of the previous Flower form, made in step 1. Close the jump ring tight (see page 84, step 5).

3 Add the second silver ring into the previous Flower form, holding the right side of the open jump ring in the right-hand pliers. The left side of the open jump ring will travel from right to left, through the three rings of the previous Flower. The left tip of the second (silver) jump ring will then go behind the first ring (copper) and travel Bottom-wise (see page 83) up through the center of the first ring. Close the jump ring tight.

4 Add the third silver ring (gold) into the previous Flower form by holding the right side of the open jump ring in the right-hand pliers. The left side of the open jump ring will travel from right to left, through the three rings of the previous Flower. The left tip of the third jump ring will then go behind the first and second rings and travel Bottom-wise up through the center of the first and second rings. Close the jump ring tight.

5 Keep assembling the bracelet, following steps 2–4, building one Flower formation onto another until you have a Mobius chain length of 7 inches. Add an S-clasp (see page 32) or a magnetic clasp (see page 130).

BEADED MOBIUS EARRINGS

The Beaded Mobius Earrings feature bead embellishments added to each Flower spiral of rings. However, unlike the Beaded Flower Bracelet (page 82), the double loop of the bead embellishment on these earrings is not part of the linear chain. You'll use three sizes of black onyx beads to create a graduated, cascading look for this design.

Tools and Materials: To make these earrings, the hand tools you will need are two flat-nose pliers and optional chain-nose pliers for getting that pesky third ring closed. The materials you will need are twenty-four 19-gauge, 3.9mm ID jump rings (ten copper, ten silver, and four gold); six 1½-inch long, 19-gauge silver headpins for double-looping bead settings; two 2-inch long, 19-gauge silver headpins for earring backs; and six round black onyx beads (two each: 8mm, 6mm, and 4mm).

Note: For a review of opening jump rings, closing jump rings, and adding/connecting jump rings, see pages 30–31. For tips for left-handers, see pages 30, 75, and 83. For Mobius chain configuration, see page 158.

1 Set all six black onyx bead embellishments (two each of 8mm, 6mm, and 4mm beads) on 19-gauge, 1½-inch headpins and double-loop each headpin with the 3.1mm jaw of the mandrel-tip pliers (see page 35).

Add the first (copper) ring onto the double loop of the 8mm bead setting, as shown.

2 Add a second copper ring to the first copper ring, and then connect the second ring to the double loop of the 6mm bead setting.

3 Allowing the 6mm bead to lay beside the 8mm bead, add a third copper ring to the second copper ring and then connect the third ring to the double loop of the 4mm bead setting.

4 Allowing the 4mm bead to lay beside the 6mm bead, add a fourth copper ring to the third ring, then add a fifth (and last) copper ring to the fourth ring.

5 Add an earring back (see page 41), connecting the small loop to the fifth copper ring.

6 Add five silver rings, one silver ring spiraling Bottom-wise (see page 83) through each of the five copper rings.

7 Add two gold rings spiraling through the top two Flower formations only. The lower three Flower formations, each connecting the double loop of a bead setting, do not have room to allow a third ring to spiral and thus remain two-ring Flower formations. Repeat steps 1–7 to make a matching earring, for a pair.

BEADED MOBIUS BRACELET

The Beaded Mobius Bracelet plays on the concept that only two rings can spiral if there is a double loop of the bead embellishment inside each Flower formation. Thus this bracelet does not have the third interwoven ring of a traditional Flower formation. Due to the quantity and placement of beads, I used longer barrel-shaped carnelian gemstones that are 13mm long and 4mm in diameter, which require a 2-inch headpin to set these longer beads.

Tools and Materials: To make this bracelet, the hand tools you will need are two flat-nose pliers, mandrel-tip pliers (3.1mm) or round-nose pliers (marked at 3.1mm diameter), and optional chain-nose pliers. For an 8-inch bracelet, the materials you will need are forty-five 2-inch long, 19-gauge silver headpins; ninety 19-gauge, 3.9mm ID silver jump rings; three 15-gauge, 5mm ID silver catch rings; forty-five 13mm carnelian barrel beads; and a silver magnetic clasp or an S-clasp.

Note: For a review of opening jump rings, closing jump rings, and adding/connecting jump rings, see pages 30–31. For tips for left-handers, see pages 30, 75, and 83. For Mobius chain configuration, see page 158.

Note: Although only silver rings and headpins were used in this bracelet, this chain pattern can be made from any single metal or mixed metals. I sometimes used different metal rings in the steps to emphasize the chain construction details.

1 Set all the 13mm barrel bead embellishments on 2-inch 19-gauge silver headpins with the 3.1mm jaw of the mandrel-tip pliers (see page 35).

Begin the Mobius chain by joining two 15-gauge, 5mm ID silver catch rings one-on-one to serve as a beginning point. Add the first silver ring (shown here in copper), connecting the catch ring to one bead setting. Add the second silver ring (shown here in copper), connecting the first ring to a bead setting. Add the third silver ring (shown here in copper), connecting the second ring to a bead setting. Continue assembling the silver rings one-on-one, allowing each to connect a bead setting, constructing an inch or two of chain pattern.

2 As the chain progresses, make sure that all the beads are being added consistently, keeping all the double-looped headpin wires angling the same way. Here, the chain is laid flat, with alternate bead settings place above and below. You can see that the double-looped headpin wires were all attached from the same direction and at the same angle.

3 I find it easier to work the rest of the chain while holding it in my left hand (right hand for left-handers). Start at one end of the chain and work in a linear direction. Add a second (silver) ring to each Flower formation. Holding the right side of the open jump ring in the right-hand pliers, the left side of the open jump ring will travel from right to left, through the two rings of the previous Flower, then go behind the first ring and travel Bottom-wise (see page 83) up through the center of the first ring, through the double loop of the bead setting and the first ring of the next Flower formation. Use flat-nose pliers to grip both sides of the open jump ring and close it tight.

4 With a pattern established, you might find it easier to assemble each two-ring spiral with a bead setting individually, rather than try to get the second rings into the already-assembled chain. To build this chain by individual two-ring spirals, start by adding the first ring through the previous two-ring spiral and add the next bead setting.

5 Add the second (silver) ring through the previous two-ring spiral, behind and up through the center of the first ring (shown here in copper), then through the double loop of the bead setting before you close this ring.

6 Before you add the next first ring (shown here in copper) and bead setting, take care that you are allowing the previously added bead setting to lay back into formation and that all the headpins spiral the same way.

Complete the beaded chain to an 7-inch length and add either a silver magnetic clasp (see page 32), as shown, or an S-clasp (see page 130).

MASCULINE MOBIUS BRACELET

This is a four-ring masculine Mobius pattern, which allows a repetition of four spiraling rings. The preceding three-ring Mobius Chain Bracelet (page 88), even when assembled from 19-gauge rings, has a slightly mannish appeal with its ropelike quality. To accentuate its manly properties, I decided to make it in a larger, 18-gauge wire thickness and to allow four rings to spiral. Allowing a fourth ring to spiral requires a larger aspect ratio (see page 27) to create a larger inside diameter of the 18-gauge jump ring. Ultimately, my goal with this project is to show women how to make a chain with weight and girth that their husbands or boyfriends would actually wear. To make this chain look heavier and more masculine, I darkened the sterling silver using a patina process (see page 20).

Tools and Materials: To make this bracelet, the hand tools you will need are two flat-nose pliers and optional chain-nose pliers. For an 8-inch bracelet, the materials you will need are 160 18-gauge, 5.5mm ID silver jump rings; three 15-gauge, 5mm ID silver catch rings; and a silver S-clasp or a magnetic clasp.

Note: For a review of opening jump rings, closing jump rings, and adding/connecting jump rings, see pages 30–31. For tips for left-handers, see pages 30, 75, and 83.

1 Start with an S-clasp (see page 32) and silver catch ring to serve as a beginning point. Add the first rings (shown here in brass), one-on-one, in a repeating pattern. If you are using a magnetic clasp, add it after the chain assembly and begin here with a paperclip.

2 Add the second (silver) ring to the Flower formation, spiraling right to left through the catch ring (or previous two ring spiral), then behind and Bottom-wise (see page 83) up through the center of the first ring and finally through the next first ring, (shown here in brass). Continue in a repeating pattern of spiraling a second ring through each of the first rings.

3 Add the third ring (shown here in brass) to the Flower formation, spiraling Bottom-wise right to left through the catch ring (or previous three-ring spiral), then behind and up through the center of the first and second rings, and finally through the next first and second rings. Continue in a repeating pattern of spiraling a third ring through each of the first and second rings.

4 Add the fourth ring (shown here in brass), spiraling right to left through the catch ring (or previous four-ring spiral), then behind and Bottom-wise up through the center of the first, second, and third rings and finally through the next first, second, and third rings of the next Flower formation. Continue in a repeating pattern of spiraling a fourth ring through each of the first, second, and third rings. Add a catch ring to the end of the chain if you are using an S-clasp. If you are using a magnetic clasp, add it now (see page 130).

Note: Once you have a pattern established, you might find it easier to just add each four-ring Flower formation individually rather than try to go back and fit the third and fourth rings in between the other Flower forms.

DUBIOUS CHAIN BRACELET

The Dubious chain is similar to the four-ring Mobius chain (page 88), using the same larger aspect ratio–sized 18-gauge jump rings and assembled in a repeating four-on-four-on-four pattern. The Dubious chain is slightly different than the Mobius chain because you will separate each four-ring spiral into two pairs, allowing two parallel rings to spiral around two other parallel rings. To make this chain look heavier and more masculine, I darkened the brass and sterling silver using a patina process (see page 20).

Tools and Materials: To make this bracelet, the hand tools you will need are two flat-nose pliers and optional chain-nose pliers. For an 8-inch bracelet, the materials you will need are 160 18-gauge, 5.5mm ID jump rings (eighty brass and eighty silver); three 15-gauge, 5mm ID brass catch rings; and a brass S-clasp or a magnetic clasp.

Note: For a review of opening jump rings, closing jump rings, and adding/connecting jump rings, see pages 30–31. For tips for left-handers, see pages 30, 75, and 83. For Dubious chain configuration, see page 159.

1 Start with an S-clasp (see page 32) and catch ring to serve as a beginning point and assemble pairs of brass rings in a two-on-two-on-two repeating pattern, until you have 2 or 3 inches of chain. If you are using a magnetic clasp, add it after chain assembly and begin with a paperclip.

2 Start at the beginning ring pair and add the third (silver) ring from right to left through the catch ring, then behind and spiraling Bottom-wise up (see page 83) through the center of the first (brass) pair, and then through the next brass pair.

3 Add the fourth (silver) ring, parallel to the third (silver) ring added in step 2, spiraling from right to left through the catch ring, then behind and Bottom-wise up through the center of the first (brass) pair of rings, but not through the center of the third (silver) ring, so the third and fourth silver rings remain parallel. Still in the same action, spiral the fourth ring through the next brass pair, to complete the first Dubious formation.

4 Move to the next pair of brass rings (following the beginning pair of brass rings) and add the third and fourth (silver) rings as you did in steps 2 and 3.

5 Continue assembling the third and fourth (silver) rings spiraling, in the same Bottom-wise manner, completing each Dubious four-ring formation individually in sequence down the entire length of the chain. When you have a 7-inch chain, add a catch ring to the end if you are using an S-clasp or add a magnetic clasp (see page 130) to complete an 8-inch bracelet.

BEADED DUBIOUS BRACELET

The Beaded Dubious Bracelet is similar to the Dubious chain (see page 97) as it uses the same four-ring Dubious formations of two parallel rings spiraling around two parallel rings. However it differs by allowing double-loop bead settings to be sequentially placed between each four-ring Dubious formation. The sequential placement of bead settings allows the jump rings used in this bracelet to come back to a smaller aspect ratio than those used in the Dubious chain. Although it uses the same size jump rings as the Beaded Flower Bracelet (see page 82), this beaded chain pattern differs from the Beaded Flower Bracelet because the bead setting's double loop will be wrapped on a larger 3.9mm mandrel jaw since you'll need a larger inside diameter to accommodate all eight rings. To accommodate this larger diameter of the bead setting's double loop, we will also need to use 2-inch headpins to set the 6mm beads. The beaded Dubious chain requires extra attention as the addition of the third and fourth rings to each Dubious formation alternates from added Bottom-wise to being added Top-wise, alternating throughout the bracelet length to keep the chain from twisting so all the beads lay flat.

Tools and Materials: To make this bracelet, the hand tools you will need are two flat-nose pliers, mandrel-tip pliers (3.9mm) or round-nose pliers (marked at 3.9mm diameter), and optional chain-nose pliers. For an 8-inch bracelet, the materials you will need are twenty-four 2-inch long, 19-gauge silver headpins; 116 19-gauge, 3.9mm ID silver jump rings; three 15-gauge, 5mm ID silver catch rings; twenty-four 6mm carnelian beads; and a silver S-clasp or a magnetic clasp.

Note: For a review of opening jump rings, closing jump rings, and adding/connecting jump rings, see pages 30–31. For tips for left-handers, see pages 30, 75, and 83. For Dubious chain configuration, see page 159.

Note: Although silver, brass, and copper rings were used in this bracelet, this chain pattern can be made from any single metal or mixed metals. I sometimes used different metal rings in the steps to emphasize the chain construction details.

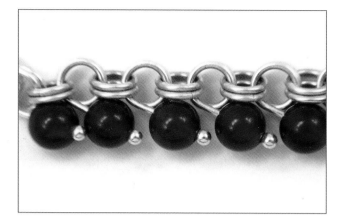

1 Start by wrapping the bead settings. Set the 6mm red carnelian beads with 2-inch, 19-gauge headpins double-looped around the 3.9mm mandrel (see page 35). Assemble the bead settings in sequence, adding two (first and second) silver rings between each double loop and keeping all the headpins angled in the same direction, as shown.

2 Add the third and fourth rings (shown here in brass) spiraling from right to left through the previous double loop, then behind and Bottom-wise (see page 83) up through the center of the first and second silver rings, and finally through the next double loop. Notice that I am only adding the third and fourth rings to *every other* connecter ring pair added in step 1.

3 Complete the connector rings pairs skipped in step 2 by adding the third and fourth rings (shown here in copper) to them, spiraling from right to left through the previous double loop, then above and Top-wise (see page 83) down through the center of the first and second (silver) rings, and finally through the next double loop. The reason for alternating the Bottom-wise and Top-wise ring placement is to keep the bead setting laying flat, without twisting, as would be the case if you set all the Dubious formations the same way. When you have completed a 7-inch chain length, add an S-clasp (see page 32) or a magnetic clasp (see page 130).

This is the finished beaded Dubious chain. Notice how the ring pairs seem to just touch and kiss between each bead setting. If you made it this far—congratulations!—this is not an easy chain pattern. However if you're a die-hard perfectionist like me, there is one further refinement you could make.

Notice carefully that every other bead setting is ever so slightly offset. The twisting of the chain may have been neutralized by alternating the Bottom-wise and Top-wise ring placement, but the beads are slightly offset due to the direction that the headpin wire was wrapped, either to the right toward the pliers handles or to the left away from the pliers handles. Hmm.

To neutralize this slight offset of the beads, you must start over and wrap half of the beads (twelve) to the right toward the pliers handles, and the other half of the beads (twelve) in the opposite spiral direction, to the left away from the pliers handles. Assemble these new bead settings so they alternate their wrapped double-loop spiral directions, while keeping all of the headpin's balls facing the same linear direction. Finally, complete each Dubious formation following steps 2 and 3.

Now, with the alternating spirals of the double loops and the alternating spirals of the Dubious formations, all the beads lay flat.

7

JAPANESE CHAINS

• •

At this point in our journey through this book, we'll shift our focus from setting beads into linear chain designs into exploring the wide, radial chain-maille patterns of the Japanese tradition. We'll take these age-old chain patterns to the next level by engineering gemstone bead settings into the chains, finding the perfect balance of metal to mineral.

"Japanese" chains are all radial patterns with multiple smaller diameter rings radiating from a center pair of rings of larger diameter that can be assembled indefinitely into a sheet of "chain maille." Japanese chains are defined by a ratio number, which describes the chain's pattern. For example, "Japanese 12-2" (the most traditional pattern) means there are twelve rings (six pair) radiating from two center rings throughout the chain-maille sheet. The Japanese 12-1 variation substitutes the typical two center rings with one ring of a larger wire thickness and diameter (in the case of the 12-1 variation, two 17-gauge, 4.75mm ID rings are replaced with one 15-gauge, 5mm ID ring).

• •

The Japanese 12-1 Triangle Key Fob assembles a 12-1 triangle pattern row by row, while the 12-1 triangle pattern is assembled from the center outward in the Triangle Mandala Choker. The next three projects—Twin Earrings, Twin Bracelet, and Triplet Bracelet—build on one another in progressive techniques of setting gemstone beads into the Japanese 12-1 chain pattern. The Twinned Tornado Bracelet project employs Tornado wire-wrapping technique to embellish Venetian glass beads that are connected with a variation on the Japanese 12-1 chain. The Japanese 8-2 Flower chain variation allows eight rings (four pair) to radiate out from a two-ring spiraling Flower formation. This chain-maille sheet will then be rolled into a round chain and set with blue quartz bead to create the Japanese 8-2 Key Fob.

HISTORICAL JAPANESE CHAIN-MAILLE PATTERNS

The Samurai warrior held a critical place in Japanese society and history from the 9th to the mid-19th century. During this history, Japanese artisans perfected the art of assembling steel jump rings into radial chain patterns for different uses, but particularly for use as protective armor (chain maille) for Samurai warriors. Lighter weaves of the Japanese 4-1 chain pattern were assembled and sandwiched between layers of cloth and leather, balancing lightweight flexibility with strength. Denser weaves of the Japanese 12-2 chain pattern were assembled into steel plate armor to protect areas that required greater flexibility, such as the armpit or elbows.

Modern artisan, good friend, and chain guru Spider has kindly donated this impressive Japanese 12-2 bracelet, crafted from 14- and 16-gauge sterling silver rings and weighing over three and a half troy ounces!

JAPANESE 12-1 TRIANGLE KEY FOB

The Japanese 12-1 chain is the simplest pattern derived from the age-old Japanese 12-2 chain. This simplified pattern allows that the two center rings be replaced by one ring of a larger wire gauge—for example, two 17-gauge, 4.75mm ID rings replaced by one 15-gauge, 5mm ID ring. As an educator, this simplification allows me to explain this pattern thoroughly as we assemble our Triangle Key Fob row by row.

Tools and Materials: To make this key fob, the only hand tools you will need are two flat-nose pliers. The materials you will need are fifteen 15-gauge, 5mm ID silver jump rings and sixty 19-gauge, 3.1mm ID silver jump rings to complete trianglar sheet.

Note: For a review of opening jump rings, closing jump rings, and adding/connecting jump rings, see pages 30–31. For tips for left-handers, see pages 30, 75, and 83. For Japanese 12-1 chain configuration, see page 159.

Note: Although this key fob is made of exclusively sterling silver rings, I sometimes used different metal rings in the steps to emphasize the chain construction details.

1 Starting with the first ring on a paperclip, assemble five single 15-gauge, 5mm rings (shown here in copper), connected by four pair of 19-gauge, 3.1mm rings (shown here in gold), creating the first row of the Japanese 12-1 triangle.

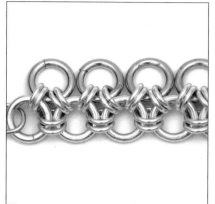

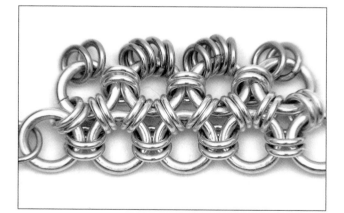

2 Add sixteen 19-gauge rings (shown here in gold) in sets of two or four onto each 15-gauge ring. (Add two rings to connect the outside 15-gauge rings in the terminating edges. Add four 19-gauge rings to the remaining 15-gauge rings, as shown.) Note that these four-ring sets will split into two pairs, connecting the first row of five 15-gauge rings with the second row of four 15-gauge rings. These rings will be shown in silver in step 3.

3 Add the second row of four 15-gauge rings (shown here in copper), each connecting through four (or two pair) of the 19-gauge rings added in step 2.

4 Add six 19-gauge rings (shown here in gold) in three pair, connecting together the four 15-gauge rings added in step 3, completing the second row of four large rings.

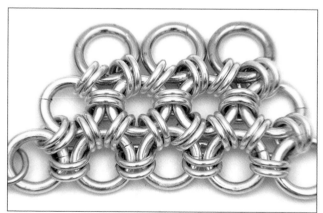

5 Add twelve 19-gauge rings (shown here in gold) to the second row of 15-gauge rings in sets of two or four onto each 15-gauge ring, as you did in step 2.

The inner four-ring set will split into two pair, connecting the second row of four 15-gauge rings with the third row of three 15-gauge rings.

6 Add the third row of three 15-gauge rings (shown here in copper), each connecting through four (or two pair) of the 19-gauge rings added in step 5.

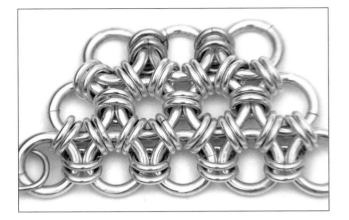

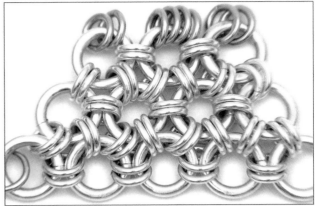

7 Add four 19-gauge rings (shown here in gold) in two pair, connecting together the three 15-gauge rings added in step 6, completing the third row of three large rings.

8 Add eight 19-gauge rings (shown here in gold) in sets of two or four onto each 15-gauge ring: one pair on each of the outside large rings as a terminating edge and four on the middle ring, as you did in steps 2 and 5.

The inner four-ring set will split into two pair, connecting the third row of three 15-gauge rings with the fourth row of two 15-gauge rings.

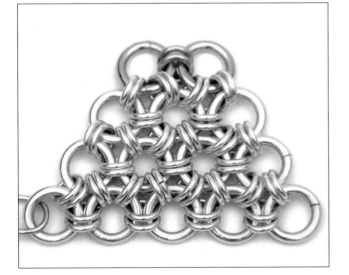

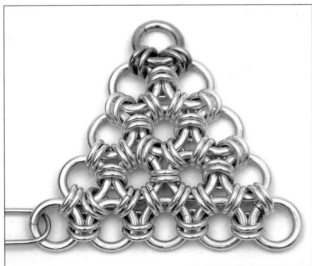

9 Add the fourth row of two 15-gauge rings (shown here in copper), each connecting through four (or two pair) of the 19-gauge rings added in step 8. Add two 19-gauge rings (shown in gold), connecting the two 15-gauge rings (shown in copper).

10 Add four 19-gauge rings (shown here in gold), two onto each 15-gauge ring of the fourth row. Complete the triangle formation with the final 15-gauge ring (shown here in copper). Finally, attach a split ring to the top of the triangle to hold your car keys.

TRIANGLE MANDALA CHOKER

This simplified Japanese 12-1 pattern replaces the two center rings of the 12-2 chain with one ring of a larger wire gauge. As an artist, this simplification facilitates the placement of specific metal rings to create patterns within the triangle shape. This Triangle Mandala Choker project features a copper triangle within a golden triangle that itself is within the overall silver triangle shape. To better control the placement of the particular metal-type rings, we'll start from the inside of the form and assemble outward.

Tools and Materials: To make this choker, the only hand tools you will need are two flat-nose pliers. The materials you will need are fifteen 15-gauge, 5mm ID jump rings (six gold-fill and nine silver); sixty 19-gauge, 3.1mm ID jump rings (six copper, twelve gold-fill, and forty-two silver); and an S-clasp or magnetic clasp. Complete the necklace by connecting the triangle mandala to two lengths of chain (Byzantine chain shown here).

Note: For a review of opening jump rings, closing jump rings, and adding/connecting jump rings, see pages 30–31. For tips for left-handers, see pages 30, 75, and 83. For Japanese 12-1 chain configuration, see page 159.

1 Connect three 15-gauge, 5mm gold rings with six (three pair) of 19-gauge, 3.1mm copper rings, as shown, creating the inner copper triangle.

2 Add twelve 19-gauge gold rings, four onto each of the 15-gauge gold rings assembled in step 1.

3 Add three 15-gauge gold rings, each connecting four (two pair) of the 19-gauge gold rings added in step 2, to complete the golden triangle.

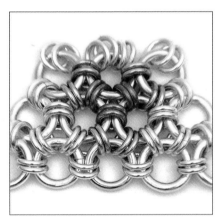

4 Add a total of twenty-four 19-gauge silver rings to the golden triangle, four to each of the six 15-gauge gold rings, as shown.

5 Connect a total of six 15-gauge rings to the outside rings of the golden triangle (step 3) with the 19-gauge silver rings added in step 4. Each 15-gauge ring is connected to adjacent 15-gauge rings with two 19-gauge rings, as shown.

6 Connect two 15-gauge rings to the top of the third row with the eight 19-gauge rings of that row. You now have a two-ring fourth row; connect the two 15-gauge rings of this fourth row with two 19-gauge silver rings. Add two 19-gauge rings to each of the 15-gauge rings you just connected, and then add a single 15-gauge ring (the fifth row) to complete the triangle.

Connect the outside rings of the five-ring row of the triangle to two chain lengths (as shown in photo on page 108) and add an S-clasp (see page 32) or a magnetic clasp (see page 130).

TWIN EARRINGS

The simplified linear chain pattern of the Japanese 12-1 chain invites gemstone bead embellishment. These Twin Earrings feature two 13mm carnelian tube beads that are set onto a length of 19-gauge wire with double loops at both ends. The Twin bead settings are then assembled with triangles of the Japanese 12-1 chain pattern to create beautiful drop earrings.

Tools and Materials: To make these earrings, the hand tools you will need are two flat-nose pliers, mandrel-tip pliers (3.1mm) or round-nose pliers (marked at 3.1mm diameter), and side cutters. The materials you will need are four 19-gauge gold wires cut into 2⅝-inch lengths; two 2-inch long, 19-gauge silver headpins for the earring backs; twelve 15-gauge, 5mm ID silver jump rings; twenty-four 19-gauge, 3.1mm ID gold jump rings; and four 13mm tube-shaped red carnelian beads.

Note: For a review of opening jump rings, closing jump rings, and adding/connecting jump rings, see pages 30–31. For tips for left-handers, see pages 30, 75, and 83. For Japanese 12-1 chain configuration, see page 159.

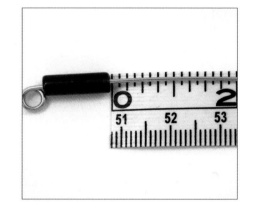

1 Use the mandrel-tip pliers' 3.1mm jaw to double-loop one end of the 19-gauge wire (see page 35). Repeat on another wire. Add one 13mm barrel-shaped red carnelian bead to each double-looped wire; you should have 1 inch of wire remaining, as shown.

2 Double-loop the opposite end of each 19-gauge wire to encase the carnelian beads. For aesthetic balance, wrap the second double loop in an opposite spiral than the first.

3 Trim off any excess wire past two revolutions with the side cutters, keeping the flat of the cutters against the bead and cutting at a 45-degree angle to the wire (see page 37). Take care to block the wire you are cutting off with your finger, to prevent the sharp wire trimming from flying across the room. Save all your metal scraps and recycle them.

4 With all the bead settings complete, gather together the 15-gauge silver rings, the 19-gauge gold rings, and two flat-nose pliers. You will add these rings to the bead settings.

Start by adding one 15-gauge (silver) ring through the double loop at one end of each bead setting. Connect these 15-gauge rings with a pair of 19-gauge (gold) rings, making sure the double-loop spirals of the bead settings spiral the same way and the beads lay parallel, as shown.

5 Add two 19-gauge gold rings to each of the now-connected 15-gauge rings. Then connect a third 15-gauge silver ring through these same four 19-gauge rings, completing the triangle formation on one end of the Twin bead setting.

6 Repeat steps 4 and 5 at the other end of the Twin bead setting to complete the opposite triangle formation. Repeat steps 1–6 to make the second earring. Add earring backs (see page 41).

TWIN BRACELET

Note: For a review of opening jump rings, closing jump rings, and adding/connecting jump rings, see pages 30–31. For tips for left-handers, see pages 30, 75, and 83. For Japanese 12-1 chain configuration, see page 159.

Note: If you are using a magnetic clasp, add it after the bracelet is assembled; use a paperclip to create a beginning point.

The Twin Bracelet features two tube-shaped gemstones set between triangles of the Japanese 12-1 chain pattern, creating a harmonic balance between symmetrical and asymmetrical elements in the linear bracelet length. Designed with the bead's shape in mind, these gemstone tubes seemed best partnered in pairs and slightly offset, which creates asymmetrical parallelograms—isn't that a fun word! Each offset parallelogram is then balanced by alternating the three-ring triangular Japanese 12-1 chain, creating a linear harmony of triangle up, parallelogram, triangle down, parallelogram, triangle up, parallelogram, triangle down, etc.

Tools and Materials: To make this bracelet, the hand tools you will need are two flat-nose pliers, mandrel-tip pliers (3.1mm) or round-nose pliers (marked at 3.1mm diameter), and side cutters. For an 8-inch bracelet, the materials you will need are ten 19-gauge gold wires cut into 2⅝-inch lengths; thirty-six 19-gauge, 3.1mm ID gold-fill jump rings; eighteen 15-gauge, 5mm ID silver jump rings; ten 13mm tube-shaped red carnelian beads; and an S-clasp or a magnetic clasp.

1 Start by making ten (five pair) double-loop bead settings; add triangle formations to each end of one bead setting (see Twin Earrings on page 110). I replaced the earring back with a gold S-clasp (see page 32) through the end of one triangle, to create a beginning point for the bracelet.

2 At the opposite triangle formation from the S-clasp (or paperclip), open the ending 15-gauge rings and add on a pair of double-looped beads, making sure the double loop spirals in the same direction and the beads lay parallel.

3 Add one 15-gauge silver ring and connect the double loop of the lower bead setting to the double loop of next bead setting, as shown. Add four 19-gauge gold rings to the top of this 15-gauge silver ring.

4 To connect the upper and lower 15-gauge rings, add one 15-gauge silver ring through the double loop of the upper bead setting and then through two of the 19-gauge gold rings added to the lower 15-gauge ring in step 3. Add two 19-gauge gold rings to the upper 15-gauge ring.

5 To complete the triangle formation, add a third 15-gauge silver ring, traveling through the four previously added 19-gauge gold rings, connecting it to the previously added 15-gauge rings. Before you close this third 15-gauge ring, connect the double loop of the next bead setting, making sure the double loop spirals in the same direction and the beads lay parallel.

6 Continue assembling each triangle formation between pairs of bead settings following steps 2–5 and remembering to alternate the triangle formations between bead settings. When you have assembled five pair of bead settings and completed the sixth triangle formation, add a catch ring for the S-clasp or add the magnetic clasp (see page 130).

For the Twin Bracelet to continue in a straight linear pattern, the Japanese 12-1 you must alternate the triangle formation from pointing down to pointing up to pointing down, etc. between each pair of bead settings. Inversely, if you want the Twin chain to bend (say, at the center of a necklace length) you would cause the triangle formations to point the same direction two or three times as needed to make the necklace length bend.

Because of the length of the carnelian tube beads, it can be problematic to adjust the bracelet length to fit. To lengthen the bracelet, one solution is to lengthen the ending three-ring triangle formation into a four-ring rectangle formation, which actually helps to pull the bracelet from opposite corners to make all the beads slightly offset. One solution to shorten the bracelet is to connect both bead settings with just a singular terminating 15-gauge ring, which would also serve as the clasp's catch ring.

In this bracelet, I replaced the red carnelian tube beads with green jade beads.

TRIPLET BRACELET

Note: For a review of opening jump rings, closing jump rings, and adding/connecting jump rings, see pages 30–31. For tips for left-handers, see pages 30, 75, and 83. For Japanese 12-1 chain configuration, see page 159.

The Triplet Bracelet takes the Twin pattern to the next level, creating a wide beaded sheet pattern. The Triplet features a six-ring Japanese 12-1 triangle formation that connects five carnelian triple bead sets, creating a bold and eye-catching bracelet design. The dynamic of this beaded chain bracelet design is complemented and completed with a triple magnetic clasp system to mimic the Triplet of gemstone beads.

Tools and Materials: To make this bracelet, the hand tools you will need are two flat-nose pliers, mandrel-tip pliers (3.1mm) or round-nose pliers (marked at 3.1mm diameter), and side cutters. For an 8-inch bracelet, the materials you will need are fifteen 19-gauge gold wires cut into 2⅝-inch lengths for double-looping bead settings; 108 19-gauge, 3.1mm ID gold jump rings; thirty-six 15-gauge, 5mm silver jump rings; and fifteen 13mm barrel-shaped red carnelian beads. For the three magnetic clasps, you will need six 1½-inch long, 19-gauge silver headpins for setting the clasps; twelvw 6mm x 1mm magnetic disk beads; and three 6mm x 6mm magnetic barrel beads.

1 Start with the finished Twin Bracelet (see page 112). Remove the S-clasp, as the two outside three-ring triangle formations of the Twin Bracelet will be expanded into a six-ring triangle formation to allow a third row of bead settings to be added parallel to the previously assembled two rows.

2 Add eight 19-gauge gold rings, four rings each onto two of the three previously added 15-gauge silver rings, as shown. Orient the bracelet so the outside triangle is pointing up (two rings on the bottom, one on top).

3 Add a fourth 15-gauge silver ring, traveling through two of the 19-gauge gold rings added in step 2, connecting to the outside silver ring at the bottom of the original triangle.

Add two 19-gauge gold rings onto this fourth 15-gauge ring.

4 Add the fifth 15-gauge silver ring, traveling through six 19-gauge gold rings, connecting the fifth ring to all three adjoining 15-gauge rings. Add two more 19-gauge gold rings onto this fifth ring.

5 To complete the triangle formation, add the sixth (top) 15-gauge silver ring, traveling through four 19-gauge gold rings, connecting the top ring to both lower 15-gauge rings. Before you close this top ring, add on a bead setting to start the third row of bead settings, making sure that the double-loop spirals all go the same direction and the beads lay parallel.

6 Move to the next three-ring triangle formation of the Twin Bracelet, which will be extended into a six-ring triangle formation.

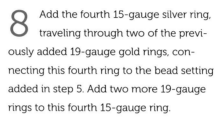

7 Add eight 19-gauge gold rings, four onto each of the top two 15-gauge silver rings.

8 Add the fourth 15-gauge silver ring, traveling through two of the previously added 19-gauge gold rings, connecting this fourth ring to the bead setting added in step 5. Add two more 19-gauge rings to this fourth 15-gauge ring.

Add the fifth 15-gauge silver ring, traveling through six 19-gauge gold rings, connecting to all three adjoining 15-gauge rings. Add two more 19-gauge gold rings onto this fifth 15-gauge silver ring.

9 Add the sixth 15-gauge silver ring, traveling through four 19-gauge gold rings, connecting to the fifth ring and the lower ring to complete the six-ring triangle formation. Before you close this sixth 15-gauge ring, add on the next third (top) bead setting, keeping the double-loop spirals all the same and making sure the beads lay together parallel.

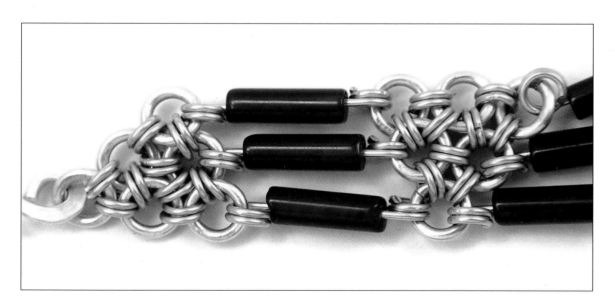

Notice that the six-ring triangle formations face in opposite directions between the Triplet bead setting, allowing the triangles to offset one another and the overall bracelet to be assembled in a linear fashion. Assemble each six-ring triangle formation of 15-gauge silver rings between Triplets of bead settings until you have assembled five Triplets of beads and the sixth six-ring triangle formation. Finish your bracelet design with a triple magnetic clasp (see next page).

TRIPLE MAGNETIC CLASP

The triple magnetic clasp is crafted by setting a series of magnetic disks that are stacked up and placed onto a silver headpin and then securely set with mandrel-tip pliers. This uniquely wide bracelet design uses three clasps side-by-side to aesthetically mimic the Triplet bead setting and to help keep the beaded sheet flat against the wrist when worn.

1 Create three magnetic clasps by following directions on page 130. All three magnetic clasps will have the same polarity when they stack side by side, as shown. Assemble one side of this triple magnetic clasping system to the ending three 15-gauge rings of the outside six-ring triangle formation, connecting each 15-gauge ring through the double loop of each magnetic clasp.

2 On the opposite end of the Triplet Bracelet, assemble the opposite side of this triple magnetic clasping system to the ending three 15-gauge rings of the outside six-ring triangle formation, connecting each 15-gauge ring through the double loop of each magnetic clasp.

When the triple magnetic clasp is connected, the ball of the headpin gets hidden inside of the barrel-shaped magnetic bead in the middle.

TWINNED TORNADO BRACELET

The Twinned Tornado jewelry design is aptly named for its combination of Tornado-wrapping technique (see page 63) and a Twin chain (see page 113), creating a visual rhythm of alternating pairs of embellished beads with Japanese 12-1 sheets. Taking all these techniques to the next level, we will double up the quantity of Venetian glass beads used and will use two lengths of 24-gauge wires to wrap each bead embellishment simultaneously. To enhance the visual rhythm we will alternate the gold and silver wires that embellish the beads and the rings in the ring pattern between the bead settings.

Tools and Materials: To make this bracelet, the hand tools you will need are chain-nose pliers, two flat-nose pliers, mandrel-tip pliers (3.1mm) or round-nose pliers (marked at 3.1mm diameter), and side cutters. For an 8-inch bracelet, the materials you will need are six 19-gauge silver wires cut into 4-inch lengths for double-looping bead settings; twelve 24-gauge silver wires, and twelve 24-gauge gold wires cut into 4½-inch lengths for wrapping beads; thirty-two 19-gauge, 3.1mm ID gold jump rings; eight 15-gauge, 5mm silver jump rings; nine 15-gauge, 5mm gold jump rings (one for a catch ring); twelve 8mm Venetian glass beads; and a gold S-clasp or a magnetic clasp.

Note: For a review of opening jump rings, closing jump rings, and adding/connecting jump rings, see pages 30–31. For tips for left-handers, see pages 30, 75, and 83. For Japanese 12-1 chain configuration, see page 159.

1 Use the mandrel-tip pliers' 3.1mm jaw to double-loop one end of the 4-inch long 19-gauge silver wire (see page 35). Add the first glass bead onto the 19-gauge silver wire. Using the tips of the chain-nose pliers, hold two 24-gauge gold wires *under* the 19-gauge silver wire at a 45-degree angle.

2 Gently wrap both 24-gauge gold wires up and around the 19-gauge silver wire, creating one full loop around the silver wire.

3 Bring the glass bead snug against the 24-gauge gold wire wrapping and bend both of the 24-gauge gold wires diagonally over the glass bead.

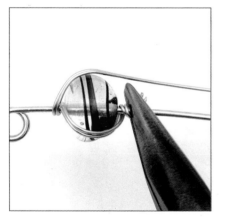

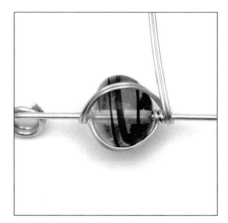

4 Wrap both of the 24-gauge gold wires one full loop around the 19-gauge silver wire and then bend them around the glass bead toward the starting point.

5 Before we wrap the next loop around the 19-gauge silver wire, we must take care of the starting tips of the wrapping wires. Bring the tips of the double wires toward the bead wrapping and trim to allow the wrapping.

6 Now that the starting tips are trimmed, wrap the 24-gauge gold wires around the 19-gauge wire for the third loop, placed just to the outside of the first loop from step 3.

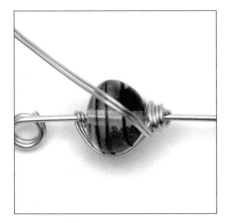

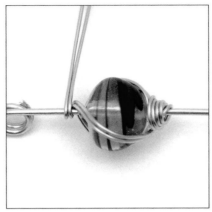

7 Wrap both 24-gauge gold wires two more times around the 19-gauge wire, angling the wire placement toward the bead to cover the first loop, creating a conical cap to the bead. Bend both wires diagonally over the glass bead and position them to balance the previous two overpasses.

8 Wrap both 24-gauge wires one full loop around the 19-gauge silver wire just to the outside of the second loop from step 5.

9 Wrap both 24-gauge gold wires around the 19-gauge wire two more times, angling the wire placement toward the bead to cover the second loop, as in step 7.

10 When you come to the end of the 24-gauge gold wires you've been bending and wrapping, wrap them one at a time and find suitable places to tuck under the wires' tips.

11 Add another bead to the 19-gauge wire.
Repeat steps 2–11, but this time use two silver 24-gauge wires. When the wrapping is complete, use the mandrel-tip pliers to double-loop the remaining 19-gauge wire in an *opposite* spiral to the first double loop made in step 1.

12 Repeat steps 1–11 creating the next double-wire-wrapped double-bead setting. Be sure to reverse the order of the wire wrapping colors, this time using silver first, gold second. Repeat steps 1–11 until you have made a total of six double-wire-wrapped double-bead settings.

13 Using four 15-gauge, 5mm rings (two gold and two silver) and eight 19-gauge, 3.1mm gold connector rings, assemble a two-on-one chain pattern (see page 38), alternating gold and silver rings, as shown.

14 Connect the first and fourth 15-gauge rings (one silver and one gold) with two 19-gauge gold rings, forming a mock four-ring Japanese 12-1 sheet—"mock" because there are no inner ring connections (yet).

Eventually, the 15-gauge gold rings will interweave, as shown. But, these rings are easier to connect (see step 16) once all the bead settings have been assembled into a linear chain (see step 15).

15 Connect the mock four-ring sheet to the double loops of the bead settings. Be sure to alternate metal colors and that the double loops spiral in one direction on the left of the sheet and the opposite direction on the right of the sheet, as shown.

16 Now you'll connect the inner parts of the four-ring sheet. Open one of the 15-gauge gold rings on the inside of the sheet (taking care not to lose any of the 19-gauge connector rings) and connect it through the other 15-gauge gold ring, as shown.

Following steps 13–16 continue assembling the bracelet, connecting three pairs of bead settings with four Japanese 12-1 four-ring sheets, until the chain is 7 inches long.

17 On one end of the bracelet, add a fifth 15-gauge ring (shown here in gold) to the four-ring sheet, to serve as a catch ring for the clasp

18 On the opposite end of the bracelet attach an S-clasp (see page 32) to the ending 15-gauge ring or add a magnetic clasp (see page 130).

Note that the interlocking of the inner parts of the 15-gauge gold rings causes the linear chain pattern to pull from opposite corners. This was purposefully done, so that each of the glass beads sits within the saddle of the double Tornado wrapping between the two beads of the opposite bead setting.

These two variations of the Twinned Tornado Bracelet create two very different looks. Having black onyx beads on a silver and gold chain feels rich and luxurious, while having red carnelian beads on a silver chain looks light and clean.

JAPANESE 8-2 FLOWER CHAIN

The Japanese 8-2 radial chain pattern allows eight rings (four pair) to radiate from two center rings; adding a twist, these two center rings spiral like a two-ring Flower formation. This radial chain pattern can be extended indefinitely into a large chainmaille sheet.

Tools and Materials: For this chain exercise, the only hand tools you will need are a pair of flat-nose pliers. The materials you will need are forty-two 19-gauge, 3.9mm ID silver jump rings and sixty-four 19-gauge, 3.1mm ID silver jump rings.

Note: For a review of opening jump rings, closing jump rings, and adding/connecting jump rings, see pages 30–31. For tips for left-handers, see pages 30, 75, and 83. For Flower chain configuration, see page 158.

Note: This chain can be made from any single metal or mixed metals. I sometimes used different metal rings in the steps to emphasize the chain construction details.

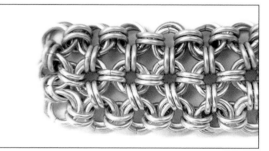

1 Start by assembling a one-on-two chain, using single 19-gauge, 3.9mm ID silver rings (shown here in copper) between pairs of 19-gauge, 3.1mm ID silver rings (shown here in gold). These rings will be shown in silver in step 3.

2 Add one 19-gauge, 3.9mm silver ring, spiraling Bottom-wise (see page 83) around each of the 19-gauge, 3.9mm silver rings added in step 1 (shown here in copper), creating a two-ring Flower form.

3 To assemble the next row of the pattern, add pairs of 19-gauge, 3.1mm silver rings (shown here in gold) to each two-ring Flower form. These rings will be shown in silver in the next step.

4 Start the second row the same as the first row (see step 1) by assembling a one-on-two chain, using one 19-gauge, 3.9mm silver ring (shown here in copper) between pairs of 19-gauge, 3.1mm silver rings (shown here in gold). These rings will be shown in silver in step 6.

5 Complete the second row the same as the first row (see step 2) by adding one 19-gauge, 3.9mm silver ring, spiraling Bottom-wise around each of the copper rings added in step 4, creating a two-ring Flower form.

6 Start the third row by adding one pair of 19-gauge, 3.1mm silver rings (shown here in gold) to the top of each two-ring Flower.

Build the third row's one-on-two chain as you did in steps 1 and 4, using one 19-gauge, 3.9mm silver ring (shown here in copper) between pairs of 19-gauge, 3.1mm silver rings (shown here in gold).

Complete the third row the same as you did in steps 2 and 5 by adding one 19-gauge, 3.9mm silver ring, spiraling Bottom-wise around each of the previously added silver rings, creating a two-ring Flower form.

JAPANESE 8-2 KEY FOB

The Japanese 8-2 Flower chain creates a unique sheet of chain-maille that can be rolled up and connected into a three-sided linear chain. For this key fob project, we will start with a sheet of Japanese 8-2 chain-maille that has eighteen two-ring Flower formations, measuring three rows tall by six columns long. Three bead settings will be added onto the end of the sheet with the seventh column of Flower formations. Finally, we will roll the sheet and connect the first and third rows of Flower formations by pairs of rings. This project creates a three-sided linear chain that terminates in a trilogy of beads at one end and a split ring to hold your car keys at the other; as aesthetically stunning as it is functional.

Tools and Materials: To make this key fob, the only hand tools you will need are two flat-nose pliers to assemble the chain and mandrel-tip pliers (3.1mm) or round-nose pliers (marked at 3.1mm diameter). The materials you will need are forty-two 19-gauge, 3.9mm ID silver jump rings; sixty-four 19-gauge, 3.1mm ID silver jump rings; three 1½-inch long, 19-gauge silver headpins; and three 10mm faceted blue quartz beads.

Note: For a review of opening jump rings, closing jump rings, and adding/connecting jump rings, see pages 30–31. For tips for left-handers, see pages 30, 75, and 83.

Note: Although this key fob is made of only silver rings, it can be made from any single metal or mixed metals. I sometimes used different metal rings in the steps to emphasize the chain construction details.

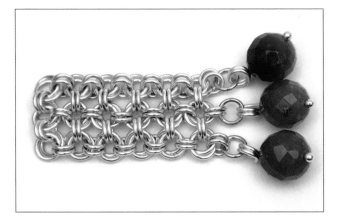

1 Start with a sheet of Japanese 8-2 Flower chain (see steps 1–6, page 124) that is three rows tall by six columns long. Make three double-looped bead settings (see page 35) using 19-gauge silver headpins and the 10mm faceted blue quartz beads.

The bead setting's double loops are assembled into the last column of the chain with single 19-gauge, 3.9mm ID silver rings (shown here in copper). These rings will be shown in silver in step 4.

2 Add three 19-gauge, 3.9mm silver rings, one each spiraling Bottom-wise (see page 83) around each of the silver rings (shown here in copper) added in step 1, creating two-ring Flower formations.

3 Add four 19-gauge silver rings (shown here in gold), in two pairs, connecting each of the Flower formations assembled in step 2. These rings will be shown in silver in step 4.

4 Roll the chain to connect the first row's *first* Flower formation to the third row's *first* Flower formation with a pair of 19-gauge, 3.1mm silver rings (shown here in gold). These rings will be shown in silver in step 7.

5 Connect the second sets of Flower formations in the first and third rows with a pair of 19-gauge, 3.1mm silver rings (shown here in gold). These rings will be shown in silver in step 7.

6 Continue connecting the Flower formations with pairs of 19-gauge, 3.1mm silver rings (shown here in gold) down the length of the chain. These rings will be shown in silver in step 7.

7 Add one 15-gauge, 5mm ID ring through the last Flower formation of the chain, and attach the split ring that will hold your keys to the ring.

The finished key fob—a blue quartz beaded triangular chain like no other.

8

THE "DOUBLE LOOP-AROUND"

· ·

In this chapter we will look at three wire-working techniques that take the double-loop bead-setting technique to the next level by leaving a wire tail that loops around the base 19-gauge wire between the bead and loop. This specialized wire-working technique, known as the "double loop-around," provides a much stronger setting of the double loop to the beads. This extra security is needed for the magnetic clasp you will learn how to make. This technique also allows the double loop of the bead setting to be angled open to seamlessly connect into the Inca Puño chain pattern in the Beaded Inca Puño Bracelet. Finally, this technique will be simplified to a "single loop-around" to set gemstone beads into the six-sided Snake chain in the Beaded Snake Chain Bracelet.

· ·

SETTING A MAGNETIC CLASP

I designed this magnetic clasp to assist my grandmothers in Missouri, who found the S-clasp difficult to maneuver. This one makes it easy for them to put on and take off their birthday present bracelets. This unique clasping system is based on wire-setting two groups of iron boron beads so they have attracting magnetic polarity—i.e., each side of the clasp has an opposite polarity. Each group of clasps consists of two or more disk-shaped beads that are stacked up and secured between the headpin's ball and a "double loop-around" wire technique. They are assembled so that the double loops are facing outward and the headpin's balls inward. A third magnetic tube-shaped bead is used between the bead settings to cover both headpin balls for an aesthetically clean, tube-shaped closure.

Note: For a review of opening jump rings, closing jump rings, and adding/connecting jump rings, see pages 30–31. For tips for left-handers, see pages 30, 75, and 83.

Tools and Materials: To make this clasp, the hand tools you will need are mandrel-tip pliers (3.1mm) or round-nose pliers (marked at 3.1mm diameter), chain-nose pliers, side cutters, measuring tape, and a felt-tip marker. The materials you will need are two 1½-inch long, 19-gauge headpins for setting the magnetic beads; four 6mm x 1mm (disk) magnetic beads; one 6mm x 4mm magnetic (tube) bead; and two 15-gauge, 5mm ID catch rings to attach your clasp.

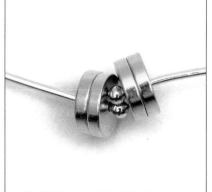

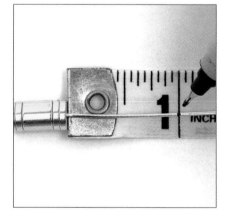

1 Add the first group of two magnetic beads onto the first 19-gauge headpin. Place the second group of two magnetic beads next to the previous group on the headpin so their sides attract, then place the second headpin through this second bead group.

2 If the bead groups are in proper magnetic attraction, the groups are attracted with the headpin's balls inward, allowing us to double loop-around the headpin wire sticking outward.

3 You will have roughly 1¼ inch of 19-gauge wire beyond the two magnetic beads. Using a fine-point felt-tip marker, mark the wire at 1 inch beyond the beads, leaving ¼ inch from this mark to the wire tip.

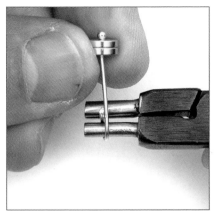

4   Grip the wire at the pen mark with the mandrel-tip pliers, keeping the 3.1mm mandrel toward you. Bend the 1 inch of headpin wire between the mark and the beads upward toward the 3.1mm jaw.

5   Bend the wire up and around the 3.1mm mandrel jaw, coiling toward the right of the wire tail, stopping before the wire goes over the next (3.9mm) mandrel jaw, as shown. When the wire reaches the top, release the pliers' pressure allowing the formed loop to rotate toward you and down to the beginning position. (For more details on how to release the pliers' pressure, see page 34).

Notice that the magnetic beads are attracted to the pliers' metal and will want to slide down the wire and get in the way. You will need to continuously keep the beads pulled back against the headpin's ball during the wrapping process.

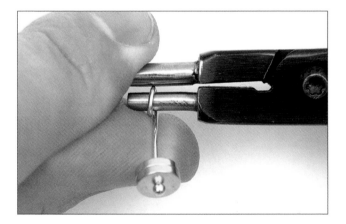

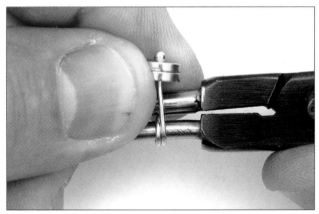

6   Relax your grip on the pliers so their jaws are not touching the 19-gauge wire, allowing the beaded headpin to rotate its single loop backward and down toward the beginning position, ready for the second bend of the double-loop setting. Re-grip and bend the wire upward, laying the new wire next to the previously wrapped wire in a tight coil.

7   When the bending wire reaches the top again, stop bending before the wire goes over the next (3.9mm) mandrel jaw, as shown.

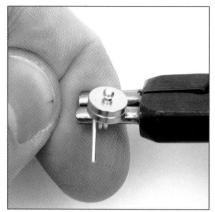

8 Relax the pliers' pressure, allowing the beaded headpin to rotate its one and a half loops back to the beginning position, ready for the third bend to complete the double-loop setting. Due to the ¼-inch wire tail, you will need to open the pliers wide to allow the full rotation back to the beginning position.

9 Re-grip and bend the wire upward in a tight coil till the wires overlap and the double loop is snug against the magnetic bead group.

10 *Note that the photographs for steps 10–19 are shot looking down on the tips of the mandrel-tipped pliers.* Grip the tip of the ¼-inch wire tail of the headpin with the chain-nose pliers and bend it downward.

11 Continue bending the wire tail around the 19-gauge base wire between the double loop and magnetic beads.

12 Bring the wire tail 180 degrees around the 19-gauge until it touches the double loop.

13 Use the tips of the chain-nose pliers to gently squeeze this loop to tighten it against the 19-gauge wire between the magnetic beads and the double loop, like a scarf around your neck.

14 Use the tips of the chain-nose pliers to grip the headpin's ball.

15 Bend the ball with the magnetic beads 30 degrees backward so that the beads hang directly under the double loop.

16 Re-grip the headpin's wire tail with the chain-nose pliers and angle it 30 degrees downward to touch the beads.

17 Bend the wire tail 90 degrees upward around the 19-gauge wire between the double loop and the magnetic beads. Use the tips of the chain-nose pliers to gently squeeze this loop to tighten it against the 19-gauge wire between the magnetic beads and the double loop, like a scarf around your neck.

18 Use the tips of the chain-nose pliers to finish the wire tail as it completes a full 360-degree wrap around the base 19-gauge wire.

19 The finished double loop-around technique, setting a two-magnetic-bead group. Complete the opposite magnetic bead group (shown here in steps 1 and 2 above) with the double loop-around, following steps 3–18. Then combine both bead settings with the center tube-shaped magnetic bead to complete the clasp. For more details, see pages 35 and 130.

BEADED INCA PUÑO BRACELET

I witnessed a local artisan crafting the Inca Puño chain while traveling throughout the Andes Mountains of southern Peru ten years ago. Interestingly, this chain pattern is also known as the Box chain in North America and the Queen's Braid throughout Europe. This unique pattern is assembled by the repetition of the knot formations to create a chain with serpentine-like flexibility. Many of the concepts for this book began with the challenge to set a gemstone bead into this repetitive pattern in a most seamless way. This pushing of the envelope opened my mind to the endless possibilities of connecting metal to mineral.

This trial and error helped me to develop the "double loop-around" wire technique, which has the strength to allow its loops of wire to be separated and angled open like the knot formation pattern of the Puño chain. I specifically chose to set a large faceted amethyst nugget that measures 15mm (⅝ inch) in length with a 12mm thickness at the center that tapers to a 7mm thickness at both ends. The large bead creates a visually weighted centerpiece into the repetitive chain and allows a perfect tapering into the 19-gauge Inca Puño chain, which has an outside diameter of 6.5mm. With this bead in mind, I specifically crafted the Beaded Inca Puño Bracelet with gold-fill wire as purple and gold visually work together and their combination speaks of a majestic aesthetic.

Note: For a review of opening jump rings, closing jump rings, and adding/connecting jump rings, see pages 30–31. For tips for left-handers, see pages 30, 75, and 83. For Inca Puño chain configuration, see page 159.

Note: Although only gold rings and clasps were used in this bracelet, this chain pattern can be made from any single metal or mixed metals. I used different metal rings in the steps to emphasize the chain construction details.

Tools and Materials: To make this bracelet, the hand tools you will need are mandrel-tip pliers (3.9mm) or round-nose pliers (marked at 3.9mm diameter), chain-nose pliers, two flat-nose pliers, side cutters, measuring tape, and a felt-tip marker. For an 8-inch bracelet, the materials you will need are two 19-gauge gold wires cut into 4¼-inch lengths for bead settings; 177 19-gauge, 3.9mm ID gold jump rings for the Inca Puño chain; four 19-gauge, 3.1mm ID gold jump rings for chain termination; two 15-gauge, 5mm ID gold jump rings; two 15mm (⅝-inch) long amethyst nuggets; and a gold magnetic clasp or an S-clasp.

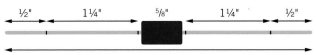

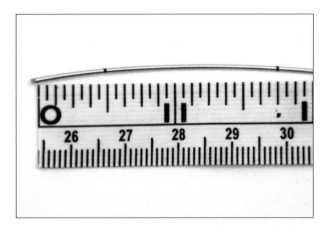

4¼-inch total wire length

SETTING THE DOUBLE LOOP-AROUND BEADS

This diagram illustrates where you will mark the 4¼-inch length of 19-gauge wire for the bead setting. From left to right, the 4¼-inch wire is divided into ½-inch wraparound + 1¼-inch double loop + ⅝-inch bead length + 1¼-inch double loop + ½-inch wraparound. You will mark the wire in steps 1 and 14.

1 Using a felt-tip marker and measuring tape, mark the 4½-inch, 19-gauge gold wire at ½ inch from the tip and then a second mark at 1¾ inches from the tip, which allows for 1¼-inch wire length to wrap a double loop on a 3.9mm mandrel. You will mark the remaining measurements in step 14, after the bead is added to the wire.

2 *Note that the photographs illustrating steps 2–13 are shot looking straight down on the mandrel-tip pliers.* Grip the wire at the first mark (½ inch from wire tip) with the mandrel-tip pliers, keeping the 3.9mm mandrel toward you.

3 Bend the 1¼ inches of wire between the first and second marks around the 3.9mm mandrel jaw, coiling toward the right of the ½-inch wire tail, stopping before the wire goes over the next (3.1mm) mandrel jaw.

4 When the wire reaches the top, relax your grip on the pliers so their jaws are not touching the 19-gauge wire, allowing the single loop to rotate backward and down toward the beginning position, ready for the second bend of the double loop setting.

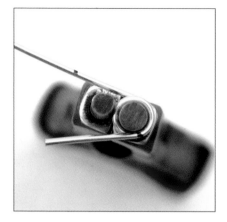

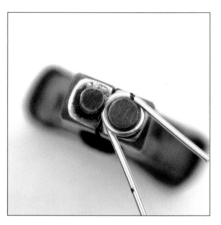

5 Re-grip the loop and continue bending the 1¼-inch wire around the 3.9mm mandrel jaw, coiling toward the right of the wire tail, stopping before the wire goes over the next mandrel.

6 Relax the pliers' pressure, allowing the one and a half wire loops to rotate back toward to the beginning position, ready for the third bend to complete the double-loop setting. Because of the ½-inch wire tail, you will need to open the pliers wide to allow the full rotation back to the starting position.

7 Re-grip the loops and continue bending the 1¼-inch wire around the 3.9mm mandrel jaw. Stop when the wires cross at a 90-degree angle and the felt-tip marks are almost touching.

8 Grip the tip of the ½-inch wire tail with the chain-nose pliers and bend it downward.

9 Continue bending the wire tail 180 degrees around the 19-gauge base wire until it touches the double loop.

10 Grip the longer part of the 19-gauge wire and bend it 30 degrees backward so that this wire comes from the aesthetic center of the double loop.

11 Re-grip the tip of the wire tail with the chain-nose pliers and bend it upward.

12 Continue bending the wire tail another 180 degrees upward and around the 19-gauge base wire, completing a 360-degree loop around it.

13 Use the tips of the chain-nose pliers to finish the wire tail by pinching it into place next to the previously wrapped wire in a tight coil. Trim and/or file as necessary so the flat surface of the gemstone bead has full aesthetic contact with this "loop-around" wire.

14 Add the 15mm nugget bead to the double-looped wire you made in steps 1–13. You should have at least 1¾ inches of 19-gauge wire remaining.

Using a felt-tip marker and measuring tape, mark the remaining wire at 1¼ inch from the bead for the double loop (wrapped on a 3.9mm mandrel) and a second mark at 1¾ inches, which allows the ½-inch loop-around length.

15 Grip the wire at the first mark (1¼ inch from the bead) with the mandrel-tip pliers, keeping the 3.9mm mandrel toward you (see steps 2–7, above).

Bend the 1¼ inch of wire twice around the 3.9mm mandrel, until the wires cross.

Note that for aesthetic balance the double loops at each end of the bead spiral in opposite directions.

16 Grip the ½-inch wire tip with chain-nose pliers and wrap it 180 degrees around the base 19-gauge wire.

17 While griping the double loop, bend the nugget 30 degrees backward so that the double loop is directly aligned with the bead.

18 Continue wrapping the ½-inch wire around the 19-gauge base wire for another 180 degrees, completing one full loop around the base wire.

ANGLED-OPEN DOUBLE-LOOP BEAD SETTING

19 Continue wrapping as needed to tighten the double loop against the bead. Trim off any excess wire with side cutters (see step 13).

1 To angle open the double loop, start by wedging one jaw of a flat-nose pliers between the loops.

2 With this wedge in place, grip the opposite wire loop with the chain-nose pliers to help open the angle slightly.

3 Once a gap is created, you can get on both sides with the tips of chain-nose pliers to stretch the double loop open.

4 Continue spreading apart the wire loops equally with the chain-nose pliers.

ASSEMBLING THE BEADED INCA PUÑO CHAIN

5 The wire loops should be angled open more than 45 degrees and less than 90 degrees.

Note: If you are unfamiliar with the repeating pattern of the Inca Puño chain, please refer to the Inca Puño chain overview in the appendix, page 159.

Note: Although only gold rings and clasps were used in this bracelet design, I used different metal rings in the steps to emphasize the chain construction details.

1 With the bead setting's double loops angled open, the Inca Puño chain can be assembled with individual jump rings in a seamless assembly of metal and mineral—gold and amethyst.

2 Add two 19-gauge, 3.9mm (silver) jump rings, each through the center of the double loops, one on each side of the loops. Hold the knot formation open with a wire, shown here in copper.

3 Add four 19-gauge, 3.9mm rings (two silver and two copper); two copper rings through the knot formation; and the two silver rings through the copper pair, creating the 2+2 pattern.

4 Fold back the pair of silver rings and angle open the pair of copper rings into a knot formation (see page 66). Hold the knot formation open with a wire, shown here in copper.

COMBINING TWO LENGTHS OF INCA PUÑO CHAIN

5 Continue assembling the Inca Puño chain on both sides of the bead embellishment, following steps 1–4 until you have three chain lengths, each seven knot formations long.

Owing to its lack of connecting pairs, it is a bit more difficult to connect two chain lengths of Inca Puño chain pattern together, but it's certainly not impossible. Here is a trick that will add two of the four rings of the knot formation in copper and then fill in the two missing rings in silver.

Note: Although only gold rings and were used in this bracelet design, I used different metal rings in the steps to emphasize the chain construction details.

1 Start with two lengths of Inca Puño chain that both end in the 2+2 open knot pattern.

2 Fold back the knot formations on the ends of each chain and place a single (copper) ring through each knot. Connect the copper rings you just added.

3 Gently twist the two chain sections in opposite directions until the single copper rings lay at the same angle as their neighboring rings of the chain pattern; these two copper rings will serve as two rings of a four-ring knot formation.

4 You will need to add the next two rings (shown here in silver) into the chain pattern without allowing the chains to untwist. The first ring (shown here in silver) will travel through two gold rings within the knot formation and then through one ring (shown here in copper) on the outside of the knot formation. The second ring (shown here in silver) will need to travel through the opposite two gold rings within the knot formation and through the opposite (copper) ring and the previously added (silver) ring on the outside of the knot formation.

REVERSING THE INCA PUÑO CHAIN PATTERN

The placement of an interwoven three-ring Flower into the ending knot formation of the chain causes the Inca Puño chain pattern to reverse as it is continued beyond the Flower formation

1 Add three 19-gauge, 3.9mm jump rings (one copper, one silver, one gold) through the ending knot formation of the Inca Puño chain to create a three-ring Flower spiral (see page 75).

2 With the Flower formation set into the Inca Puño chain, add the next knot formation by adding four 19-gauge, 3.9mm ID rings, assembled two-on-two (in copper and silver), as shown.

3 Fold back the silver rings and angle-open the copper rings to create a knot formation beyond the Flower formation, continuing the Inca Puño chain. Hold the knot formation open with a wire, shown here in brass.

Note: Although only gold rings and were used in this bracelet design, I used different metal rings in the steps to emphasize the chain construction details.

1 With the Inca Puño chain continued on both sides of the three-ring Flower formation, you can see how the knot formations angle away from the center Flower form in opposite directions.

2 To terminate the Inca Puño chain length, add two 19-gauge, 3.1mm diameter ring pairs (shown here in silver) to each end of the chain through their ending knot formations. These smaller-diameter rings are used to taper the chain and keep the ending knot formations tight so they won't unfold.

3 To connect the forged S-clasp (see page 32) add one larger 15-gauge, 5mm ring (shown here in silver) to each end of the chain through the smaller-diameter ring pairs you added in step 2.

4 To complete the bracelet in an all gold theme, replace the tapering (silver) ring pairs added in step 2 and the connecting (silver) ring added in step 3 with gold-fill rings, and attach a gold-plated magnetic clasp (see page 130), as shown.

The Inca Puño chain section between the beads and clasp has a reversing Flower formation in the middle with seven Puño knot forms on each side to create an 8-inch bracelet.

A single amethyst bead provides a vivid focal point against the silver chain in this variation of the Beaded Inca Puño Bracelet.

EUROPEAN 4-1 RHOMBUS KEY FOB

The European 4-1 is a very basic chain-maille pattern that was woven into shirts of armor for Renaissance knights to wear as protection from sword and lance blows. It is assembled by alternating rows of angled rings that connect one-on-one, in four directions. For the key fob, you will assemble the European 4-1 in a radial scheme, adding rings to the outside of the form to create a rhombus-shaped chain-maille sheet. This limited introduction to the Euro 4-1 chain pattern is necessary because it is the basis of the Beaded Snake Bracelet project (page 146).

Tools and Materials: To make this key fob, the hand tools you will need are two flat-nose pliers. The materials you will need are twenty-four 15-gauge, 5mm ID jump rings plus a split ring to hold your car keys. For the bi-metal look, use twelve rings each of silver and gold.

Note: For a review of opening jump rings, closing jump rings, and adding/connecting jump rings, see pages 30–31. For tips for left-handers, see pages 30, 75, and 83. For European 4-1 chain configuration, see page 159.

Note: Although gold and silver rings were used in this key fob, it can be made from any single metal or mixed metals. I used different metal rings in the steps to emphasize the chain construction details.

1 Start with five 15-gauge, 5mm rings, combining four silver rings onto one gold ring.

2 Add four 15-gauge, 5mm gold rings (shown here in copper) to connect all the silver rings. Notice that these rings angle the same direction as the center gold ring. These four rings are shown in gold in the photographs for steps 3, 4, and 5.

3 Add eight silver rings (shown here in copper), two from each outer gold ring added in step 2. Notice that these rings angle the same direction as the silver rings added in step 1. These eight copper rings are shown in silver in the photographs for steps 4 and 5.

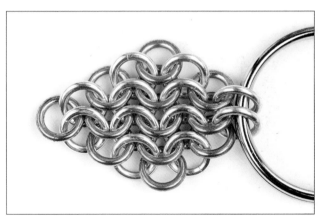

4 Add six gold rings (shown here in copper) connecting the eight silver rings added in step 3. Two of these added (gold) rings connect two silver rings at the top and bottom of the rhombus. Four of these added (gold) rings connect three silver rings on the right and left sides of the rhombus. The rhombus-shaped chain-maille sheet is now complete. Notice these added rings angle the same direction as the gold rings.

5 Add one gold ring to connect the two silver rings on the left side of the rhombus. Add a split ring to hold your keys through the two silver rings on the right side of the rhombus.

BEADED SNAKE CHAIN BRACELET

The Snake chain is based on a sheet of the European 4-1 that is rolled up into a six-sided round chain, also know as "Round maille," the "Star Weave," and "Hexagon" chain. The age-old European 4-1 sheet (page 144) is assembled by alternating rows of angled rings that connect one-on-one, in four directions. The European 4-1 chain-maille sheet is transformed into a round chain by assembling a five-row sheet of it that is rolled up and connected on both sides with a sixth row of rings into a six-sided Snake chain. To set the trio of blue quartz beads into this chain pattern I had to redesign the wire-bending method by employing a "single loop-around" technique to create a seamless connection of metal and mineral.

Tools and Materials: To make this bracelet, the hand tools you will need are mandrel-tip pliers (3.5mm) or round-nose pliers (marked at 3.5mm diameter), chain-nose pliers, two flat-nose pliers, side cutters, measuring tape, and a felt-tip marker. For an 8-inch bracelet, the materials you will need are nine 19-gauge wires cut into 2¼-inch lengths (three gold and six silver) for setting beads; a length of wire (any metal, any gauge) for trapping the bead settings; 248 19-gauge, 3.5mm ID jump rings (124 each in silver and gold); nine 6mm faceted blue quartz beads; two 15-gauge, 5mm ID silver rings; and a gold S-clasp or a magnetic clasp.

Note: For a review of opening jump rings, closing jump rings, and adding/connecting jump rings, see pages 30–31. For tips for left-handers, see pages 30, 75, and 83. For European 4-1 chain Configuration, see page 159.

Note: Although silver and gold wires and jump rings were used in this bracelet, this chain pattern can be made from any single metal or mixed metals. I sometimes used different metal rings in the steps to emphasize the chain construction details.

SETTING THE "SINGLE LOOP-AROUND" BEADS

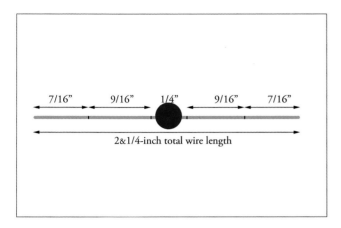

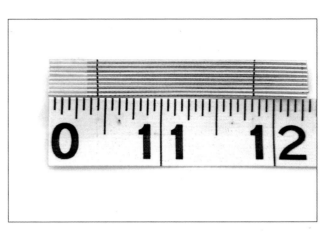

This diagram illustrates the 2¼-inch wire with marks for the appropriate spacing on both sides of the bead in the center. From the left to right, the 4¼-inch wire is divided into $^7/_{16}$-inch wraparound + $^9/_{16}$-inch single loop + ¼-inch bead length + $^9/_{16}$-inch single loop + $^7/_{16}$-inch wraparound.

1 Cut nine lengths of 19-gauge round wire (three gold and six silver), each at 2¼-inch lengths.

Using the felt-tip pen, mark each 19-gauge wire (shown here in silver) at $^7/_{16}$ inch (11mm) from both wire tips.

Note: You can expedite this process by taping all nine wires together and marking them simultaneously with a ruler.

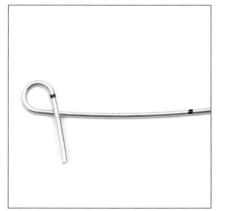

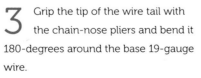

2 Grip the wire at one of the $^7/_{16}$-inch marks with the mandrel-tip pliers, keeping the 3.5mm jaw toward you. Bend the longer length of wire around the pliers' jaw, creating a single loop so both wires overlap.

3 Grip the tip of the wire tail with the chain-nose pliers and bend it 180-degrees around the base 19-gauge wire.

4 Add a 6mm bead onto the 19-gauge wire. You should have roughly 1 inch (19mm) of 19-gauge wire beyond the bead with a mark at $^9/_{16}$ inch beyond the bead, allowing you to form the 3.5mm single loop on the other side of the bead.

5   Grip the wire with the mandrel-tip pliers at the second mark, keeping the 3.5mm mandrel jaw toward you. Bend the wire between the second mark and the bead into a single loop, in an opposite spiral to the first single loop made in step 2. Keep the bend consistent so that you create a symmetrical S-curve shape. Notice that the second wire tail overlaps the base wire on the topside of the base wire, just as the tail of the first loop did.

6   Grip the tip of the second wire tail with the chain-nose pliers and bend it 180 degrees around the base 19-gauge wire. Notice that the second single loop should *not be* snug against the 6mm bead. This slight gap will be filled with the wire tails on both sides of the bead to tighten and set it.

7   Hold each loop individually with the mandrel-tip pliers and bend the loop 30 degrees backward so that the loops are centered with the bead, as shown.

8   Grip each loop individually with the mandrel-tip pliers and use the tips of the chain-nose pliers to bend each wire tail upward, filling the gap between the bead and loop.

9   Keep bending both wire tails equally, a ¼ turn at a time, to keep the bead centered.

10   Grip each loop with your fingertips and bend the single loops downward at a 30-degree angle. This will be necessary for a seamless connection into the Snake chain.

11 Grip each loop individually with the mandrel-tip pliers and continue bending the wire tail around to fill the gap between the bead and loop.

12 Use the side cutters to trim off the excess wire tails, as necessary (see page 37).

Here is a finished single loop-around set bead. You will need nine bead settings for the bracelet: three beads set with gold wire (for the center of chain pattern) and six beads set with silver wire (three for each side of the chain pattern).

ASSEMBLING THE BEADED SNAKE CHAIN

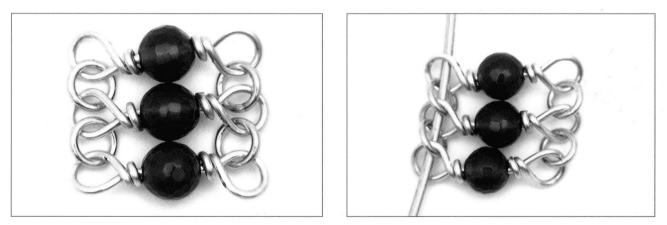

Note: Although silver and gold wires and jump rings were used in this bracelet, I sometimes used different metal rings in the steps to emphasize the chain construction details.

1 Combine three bead settings with four singular 19-gauge, 3.5mm gold rings, two on each side, as shown.

2 Trap one side of the bead settings' single loops with a length of 16-gauge wire, shown here in copper.

3 Add the next column of three singular silver rings (shown here in copper), parallel to the single loops, connecting the two gold rings added in step 1. These three copper rings will be shown in silver in the next photograph.

4 Add the next column of two singular gold rings (shown here in copper) parallel to the gold rings added in step 1, connecting the three silver rings added in step 3. The two copper rings will be shown in gold in the next photograph.

5 Add the next column of three singular silver rings (shown here in copper), parallel to the three silver rings added in step 3, connecting the two gold rings added in step 4. These three rings will be shown in silver in the next photograph.

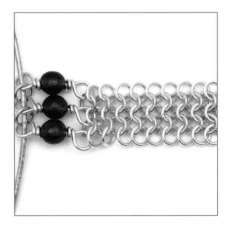

6 Add the next column of two singular gold rings (shown here in copper), parallel to the gold rings added in step 4, connecting the three silver rings added in step 5. These two rings will be shown in gold in the next photograph.

7 Continue alternating three silver and two gold rings in the European 4-1 pattern, following steps 3–6.

8 Add a total of eighteen columns of rings, or roughly 1¾ inch of European 4-1 pattern.

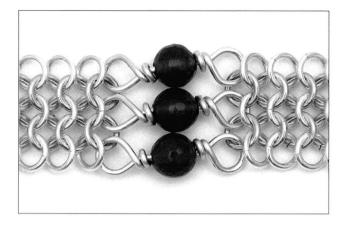

9 Repeat steps 1–8 on the other (left) side of the triple-bead embellishment. You should now have two European 4-1 sheets of equal lengths, one on each side of one silver bead setting.

Repeat steps 1–9 with the remaining three beads set in silver wire. You now have the two halves of the chain, which will each be connected to the three gold bead settings that will become the center of the bracelet.

10 You'll now assemble the two halves of the beaded chain made in steps 1–9 and the three *gold* bead settings made on pages 147–149. Add two singular rings (shown here in copper), connecting the left side of the three bead settings to the chain's ending pair of gold rings, keeping the added rings parallel to the chain's silver rings.

11 Assemble the other half of the beaded chain length to the right side of the three gold bead settings as you did in step 10. The connector rings shown in copper in steps 10 and 11 will be shown in silver in step 12.

12 Add in the third ring (shown here in copper) to complete the columns on both sides of the gold wire-wrapped bead settings. This ring will connect to the single loop of the top bead setting as the sheet is rolled into a round chain.

The previously added silver rings (shown here in copper) are connected to the single loop of the top bead setting on both sides as the Euro 4-1 flat sheet is gently rolled into a round chain that will become the six-sided Snake chain.

13 We will now "zip up" the Snake chain by adding the sixth row of singular gold rings (shown here in copper) to connect the silver rings of the first and fifth rows of the European 4-1 chain. This added sixth row transforms the static flat sheet of European 4-1 into the six-sided Snake chain.

14 Continue adding singular gold rings (shown here in copper) to connect the sixth (outside) rows of *all four* flat chain lengths, creating *four* Snake chain lengths between the *three* Triplet bead settings.

FINISHING THE BEADED SNAKE CHAIN BRACELET

Continue the Snake chain until both ends finish with the nineteenth column (three gold rings), as shown.

Note: Although silver and gold wires and jump rings were used in this bracelet, I sometimes used different metal rings in the steps to emphasize the chain construction details.

1 Add three silver rings (shown here in copper) to the end of the chain. Two of these three rings are added in the same Snake pattern, connecting two gold rings and laying parallel to the previous silver rings. The third silver ring (shown here in copper) is added in a very odd way: It does not connect any gold rings; instead it goes through the center of the chain and connects to the silver ring, as shown. Repeat at the other end of the chain.

2 Connect the two silver rings added in step 1 with two gold rings (shown here in copper). Repeat at the other end of the chain.

3 Add two gold rings (shown here in copper) through the odd silver ring added in step 1. Repeat at the other end of chain.

4 At one end of the chain, add one silver 15-gauge, 5mm ring (shown here in gold) through all four rings added in steps 2 and 3, above. The S-clasp (see step 5) will hook into this ring to close the bracelet.

5 At the opposite end of the chain, add another 15-gauge, 5mm silver ring through all four rings added in steps 2 and 3, above. Add a gold S-clasp (see page 32) to this ring.

The use of red carnelian beads and silver rings in the chain give this bracelet a vintage feel.

APPENDIX

Here we will delve a bit more deeply into working with Argentium silver, and I'll teach you how to make your own headpins using a simple teardrop technique. The illustrated chain configurations are a quick visual reference to all the chain patterns used in the jewelry pieces in this book, and since they are presented all in one layout, it will be easy for you to identify the differences and similarities among the chains and the special characteristics of each chain.

WORKING WITH ARGENTIUM SILVER

Argentium sterling silver, invented by Peter Johns in 1996, is a relatively new silver alloy that lends silversmithing numerous benefits over traditional sterling silver. A thin layer of germanium oxide, creates a barrier that decreases reticulation (wrinkling) of the metal's surface, so that heated Argentium wire pulls up into a perfectly smooth teardrop-shaped ball. This teardropping technique allows the studio jeweler to create aesthetically pleasing headpins from any gauge of Argentium sterling silver wire.

HARDENING WIRE WITH REPEAT BENDING

Half-hard 19-gauge Argentium sterling silver wire feels a bit too soft off the coil, so I harden and straighten the wire by bending it slightly with repeated pulls, see page 26. Start by uncoiling 3 feet of wire and hold one end with the flat-nose pliers in your nondominant hand. With your dominant hand, pull on the wire using a folded bandana to reduce friction (see page 26). Start each pull at the pliers and pull evenly to the wire's end. With each pull, adjust your thumb's position to make the wire bend against its original curve. With the

final few pulls, equalize the thumb-to-first-finger pressure so the wire is pulled straight. After a dozen pulls, the wire should be straight and quite a bit springier than before.

CUTTING WIRE LENGTHS

To cut multiple 4½-inch, 19-gauge wires, I use a measuring tape and side cutters. Beginning at one end of the straightened wire, measure 4½ inches and cut with the side cutters. Use this 4½-inch cut length as your template for cutting the remaining 4½-inch lengths.

Note: The 4½-inch wire will become a 4-inch length after you teardrop each end, and will be cut into two 2-inch headpins. A 3½-inch wire will be a 3-inch length after teardropping, and will be cut into two 1½-inch headpins.

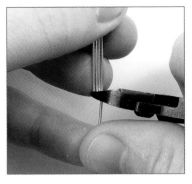

HANDCRAFTING TEARDROPPED HEADPINS

Your immediate workspace should be equipped with your torch, lighter, pliers, a pile of 19-gauge Argentium sterling silver wires, and a warm metal or stone, non-burnable surface to lay down the hot wire. I also recommend dimming the lights to better see the subtle color changes of the Argentium sterling silver at it transforms from a solid to a liquid state.

With your pliers in your dominant hand, hold the middle of the wire length and bring the tip of the wire to the tip of the blue flame and count slowly: 1 . . . 2 . . . 3 . . . After about three seconds, you will see the wire turn orange

and make a quick flash of liquid shine as it melts and is pulled upward and swells in size, forming a teardrop at the end of the wire. The trick here is to pull the wire out of the flame as soon as that intense orange flash

Propane Torch

I use a hardware store propane torch, mainly because I'm cheap, but I have never felt the need for a proper oxyacetylene jeweler's torch. Besides, a propane torch works better for this technique because I want to bring the wire to a stationary flame rather than the conventional technique of bringing the flame to the metal. However, if you do have an oxyacetylene torch, attach the hand piece to a vertical support to keep the flame stationary.

Torch Precautions

If you have any worries about using a hot torch, please seek advice and demonstration from your local handyman or hardware store. Beyond these basics, please take the following precautions:

1. You must hold the wire you are heating in a pair of pliers, or, as the wire heats up, it will burn your fingers.
2. Repetitive teardropping can cause the heat to conduct through the pliers and start to melt the plastic handle guards, so switch out pliers when they get warm.
3. Melting any metal gives off toxic fumes that are hazardous to your mental and physical well-being. Please work in a well-ventilated studio. I use an 8-inch fan that blows across my face when I work with a torch.

appears. As the teardrop cools another three seconds, keep the wire vertical, bead end down, so that the wire behind the teardrop does not bend to one side.

To teardrop the other end of the wire you will need to turn your pliers over 180 degrees so the previous teardrop is now pointing upward. Repeat the three-second heating process above to teardrop the opposite wire end. Allow the teardrop to cool for another three seconds. Keep the wire vertical, bead end down, so that the wire behind the teardrop does not bend to one side. Place the heated, and still quite hot, double-teardropped wire down on a warm non-burnable surface, such as Solderite or ceramic, and let it cool slowly. Do not try to quench the wires in water or set them down on a cold surface, as the thermal shock will cause the teardrops to pop off the wire.

Notice that the overall length of the double-teardropped wire is now roughly 4 inches, due to melting silver being pulled up into the diameter of the teardrop shape.

FINISHING TEARDROPPED HEADPINS

Before we make earrings or set gemstones with our new headpins, let's heat treat them in the oven (see page 19), clean them of oxidation by pickling (see page 19), and polish them to a brilliant shine in a steel-shot tumbler (see page 20).

These procedures prepare the headpins so they can be used to set beads with a double loop (see page 35) or to bend into earring hooks (see page 41) without any further heat treating or polishing necessary. Finishing your headpins before you assemble them into jewelry is important because some semiprecious stone beads are damaged by the above heating and polishing techniques. Also, magnetic beads lose their polarity during heating, and soft minerals like turquoise and lapis lazuli can burn in the heating process and lose their shine in the tumble.

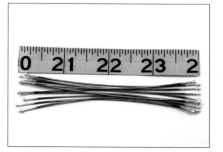

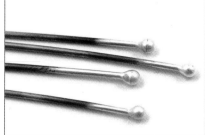

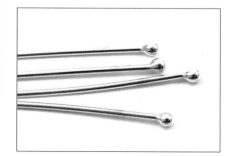

RESOURCES

Wire Suppliers

Rio Grande in Albuquerque, NM
1-800-545-6566
www.riogrande.com
(noble and base metal wire—gold, silver,
copper, brass, and bronze)

Hauser & Miller in St. Louis, MO
1-800-462-7447
(noble metal wire—golds and silvers)

E. B. Fitler in Milton, DE
1-800-346-2497
(base metal wire—copper, brass,
and bronze)

Bead Suppliers

Rio Grande in Albuquerque, NM
1-800-545-6566
www.riogrande.com

Fire Mt. Gems in Grants Pass, OR
1-800-423-2319
www.firemountaingems.com

House of Gems
www.houseofgems.com

Earthstone
www.earthstone.com

Bonita Creations
www.bonitacreations.com

Magnetic Arts
www.magneticarts.net

Handtool Suppliers

Rio Grande in Albuquerque, NM
1-800-545-6566
www.riogrande.com
(exclusive retailers for Swanstrom Pliers)

Otto Frei in Oakland, CA
1-800-722-3456
www.ottofrei.com

Jewelry Supply
www.jewelrysupply.com

Progress Tool
www.progresstool.com

Precut Jump Rings

APAC Tool in Providence, RI
1-401-724-6090
www.apactool.com
(kerf-less jump rings, headpins, s-clasps,
and my supply kits)

Spider Chain in San Francisco, CA
1-510-368-0646
www.spiderchain.com
(saw-cut jump rings in multiple
metals and sizes)

Headpins, S-Clasps and Magnetic Clasps

APAC Tool in Providence, RI
1-401-724-6090
www.apactool.com
(19-gauge headpins, jump rings, s-clasps,
magnetic clasps and my supply kits)

Rotary Tumbler

Lortone Tumblers in Mukilteo, WA
1-425-493-1600
www.lortone.com

Three-Prong Chuck

David Chain Jewelry
www.davidchain.com/toolkit.html

Publications

Art Jewelry
www.artjewelrymag.com

Lapidary Journal Jewelry Artist
www.lapidaryjournal.com

American Craft Magazine
www.craftcouncil.org

Author Contact

Scott David Plumlee
P.O. Box 192, Arroyo Seco, NM 87514
www.davidchain.com
Email: info@davidchain.com
www.davidchain.com/links.html

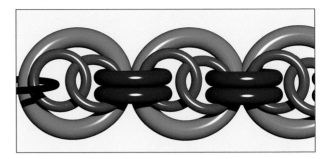

Simple 1+2+1+2 Chain

Infinity Chain

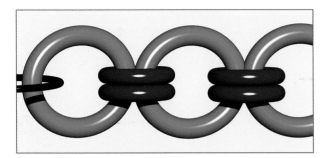

Byzantine Chain—open knot form

Byzantine Chain—folded knot form

Flower Chain

Flower formation—3 rings

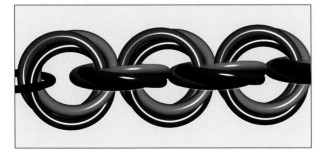

Mobius Chain

Flower Formation—4 rings

Dubious formation—4 rings

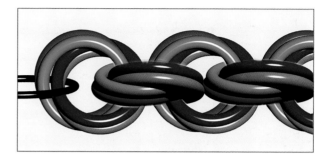

Dubious Chain

Japanese 12-1 formation

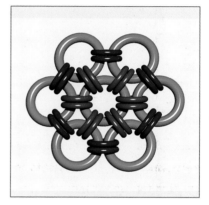

Japanese 12-1 Chain Maille

Inca Puño—open knot form

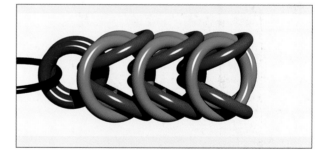

Inca Puño—folded knot form

European 4-1 formation

European 4-1 Chain Maille

INDEX